Innovation Diffusion in the New Economy

This book gives an overview of the theories of tacit knowledge and explains how this relates to a background of philosophical, neurological and pedagogic literature. The authors explain the importance of tacit knowledge for evolutionary models of innovation and give an overview of the field of organisation thinking, which uses this in order to open up questions of the new role of tacit knowledge as the processes of economic and social change are accelerated by new market and technological pressures.

Barbara Jones is a Research Fellow in Manchester Business School (University of Manchester), and a member of the European Work and Employment Research Centre.

Bob Miller is a Research Associate in Manchester Business School (University of Manchester).

Routledge Advances in Management and Business Studies

Innovation Diffusion in the New Economy

The tacit component

Barbara Jones and Bob Miller

LONDON AND NEW YORK

First published 2007
by Routledge
2 Park Square, Milton Park, Abingdon, Oxon, OX14 4RN

Simultaneously published in the USA and Canada
by Routledge
270 Madison Ave, New York NY 10016

Routledge is an imprint of the Taylor & Francis Group, an informa business

Transferred to Digital Printing 2008

© 2007 Barbara Jones and Bob Miller

Typeset in Times New Roman by
Keystroke, 28 High Street, Tettenhall, Wolverhampton

British Library Cataloguing in Publication Data
A catalogue record for this book is available from the British Library

Library of Congress Cataloging in Publication Data
Jones, Barbara.
  Innovation diffusion in the new economy : the tacit component / Barbara Jones
and Bob Miller.
    p. cm. – (Routledge advances in management and business studies series)
  Includes bibliographical references and index.
  1. Diffusion of innovations. 2. Technology transfer. 3. Tacit knowledge.
I Miller, Bob, 1954– II. Title.
  HC79.T4J66 2007
  338′.064–dc22   2006024244

ISBN10: 0–415–31047–4 (hbk)
ISBN10: 0–415–48807–9 (pbk)
ISBN10: 0–203–41709–7 (ebk)

ISBN13: 978–0–415–31047–5 (hbk)
ISBN13: 978–0–415–48807–5 (pbk)
ISBN13: 978–0–203–41709–6 (ebk)

Contents

Foreword

Tacit knowledge, or, as you will soon learn, tacit knowing is an emerging science that will have a profound impact on human capital and organisation performance management. The scholarly authors have made a valiant attempt to provide thought-leaders with the 'facts' about tacit knowledge, and an understanding of interesting and useful research.

The demand signal for this book is simple. Organisations are expanding at record levels, outsourcing work to knowledge workers in various places around the globe, and are struggling with processes by which to understand, capture and utilise *all* types of worker knowledge. As you will learn, *all* is an important descriptor, and some will be surprised by the types of knowledges incumbent workers possess.

Leaders realise that innovation and technology improve organisational performance and expands human knowledge, experience and process awareness, all of which are used to improve worker productivity. Organisations that fail to capture new and emerging knowledges to leverage innovation will have wasted a great opportunity to maintain their competitive advantage. Hence the operational challenge.

Valuable human and knowledge resources will be wasted unless organisations make better use of *all* types of knowledge resources. Tacit knowledge in particular is still considered to be relatively unexplored, and proper understanding and management of this resource are of immense importance for better organisational performance.

How will future leaders know and understand a worker's knowledge capacity? Is that capacity limited to current assignments? Can that type of knowledge be transferred to another assignment? How will this knowledge be assessed and used to predict performance? These and many other questions will be addressed.

High-performance organisations are continuously looking for that competitive edge, and this book is the beginning of that journey.

Michael L. Brown
Founder and CEO
SkillsNET Enterprises

Acknowledgements

Access to the Harper Torchbook edition of *Personal Knowledge* was facilitated by Mrs Sheila Mills, librarian of Regent's Park College, Oxford, the location of the only UK COPAC holding of this title.

1 Introduction

Why tacit knowledge?
Why this book?

The argument

This book will attempt to establish three clusters of assertions:

- That Michael Polanyi's theory of personal knowledge and tacit knowing, which has become widely known under the unfortunate and misleading rubric of 'tacit knowledge', is an important contribution to an evolutionary, bottom-up understanding of all human knowledge and action. That attempts to make his work immediately relevant have resulted in a number of unfortunate dichotomies of knowledge, as if Michael Polanyi were only claiming the existence of a newly discovered area of knowledge alongside those already recognised. That this in turn has led to unnecessary and fruitless attempts to generate new knowledge by establishing channels for the conversion and communication of knowledge between supposedly different types of knowledge. That we need to escape this impasse by accepting that knowledge is always contextual and is always used as part of a skill. Our conclusions lead to the suggestion that we should abandon the much-abused terminology of 'tacit knowledge' and equally not stop at Polanyi's more used term 'tacit knowing', but that from the point of view of skills we should speak, still in Polanyi's words, of the 'tacit component' or 'tacit coefficient' of all skill, including the skills of formulating and communicating ideas. We suggest that the successful identification and diffusion of new skills is inseparable from identifying and mapping the tacit component of these skills. Polanyi's work already identifies a number of the elements of this component, on the basis of which we should be able to begin to classify those active in different kinds of skill.
- That Joseph Schumpeter's theory of innovation as the only source of economic growth is becoming increasingly relevant as globalisation opens all markets to new entrants and competition eats away at all quasi-rents and market niches. That the resource-based theory of the firm and of competitive advantage associated with Edith Penrose and Michael Porter captures much of the reality of the processes by which all inputs available on the market become interchangeable while only those generated within

the firm itself ensure a precarious competitive edge. That, as Peter Drucker later emphasised, the only asset of the firm which cannot be easily replicated by competitors is knowledge. That, as argued by Nelson and Winter (1982), the most valuable knowledge of a firm is that which is embodied in routines and in teams which can both carry out and replicate, develop and innovate routines. That since ultimately even routines can be replicated by competitors – by poaching staff, by reverse engineering and by industrial espionage – the only secure form of competitive advantage is that embodied in constant incremental improvement and innovation. That Polanyi's understanding of knowing as a continuous process of discovery becomes especially relevant in processes of continuous incremental innovation. That mapping the tacit coefficient and tacit component evolving in new forms of work, developed at the site of ongoing incremental improvement, is important both for the effective diffusion of new skills and for their further improvement.

- That Polanyi's ideas have another quite different field of application in the simultaneous processes of despatialisation brought about by the advent of cyberspace. Polanyi's concepts of physiognomic recognition, the prosthetic function of heuristics, the indwelling of our contexts, the turning around of established schemas as the basis for new conceptualisations, and the tacit integration of all of these processes have enormous relevance for the ways in which the flood of information which we absorb through cyberspace can begin to make sense to us. The servicing and use of the hardware and software of cyberspace in itself creates enormous new bodies of so-called 'tacit knowledge' embedded in skills. More important than this is the contribution which Polanyi can make to understanding how the cyber-mediated world can be real for us. This is relevant to information about markets, products, fashions and the effect of wider social trends on the economy. The active integration of information absorbed through new media will lead to a revolution in sensibilities comparable to that produced by the printing press and mass literacy. The way in which this active integration is achieved by experience and in Polanyi's terms by *indwelling*, in combination with the drive towards constant innovation within businesses, means that there is a problem with the encapsulation of new knowledge within firms and the creation of 'skills escalators' which exclude those without access to these ongoing developments. However, a countervailing trend is present in the technical imperatives to restandardise systems to ensure interconnectability, and in the commercial processes which lead to the emergence of new standard products and techniques (an aspect of Schumpeter's 'creative destruction'). The identification of the generic skills which will be at the core of future skills landscapes is therefore of great significance to those bodies which wish to achieve national, regional or sectoral competitive advantage by taking advantage of clustering and spillover.

Michael Polanyi and tacit knowing

Michael Polanyi developed his concept of tacit knowing, usually referred to in business-oriented literature under the rubric of 'tacit knowledge' (drawing especially on Polanyi 1966), as part of a much wider philosophy, most of which is not usually referred to by writers who use the concept.[1] He saw tacit knowing as an irreducible part of personal knowledge. The part of his theory which is most widely known and transmitted states that the greatest part of our knowledge of the world is necessarily inexplicit. The reason for this is that we focus on only a small part of the world at any time, while all of our background knowledge of the rest of the world, while necessary for our unconscious and subconscious calculation of our actions in relation to the world, must remain implicit in order not to distract us from the focus of our conscious attention. Whatever we learn about the world, those things which we learn by deliberate instruction, as well as those which we acquire by subliminal familiarity, become part of our fund of personal knowledge. Tacit knowing is therefore not reducible to that part of knowledge which arises within and is drawn on in specific specialist contexts. There is a core of personal knowledge in every life situation and every practice, no matter how ubiquitous and universally applicable it may be. Tacit knowing is sometimes perceived to be specific to special kinds of situations because it is often in the confrontation of individuals with different experience that conflicting assumptions rooted in different funds of tacit knowledge may be exposed.

One consequence of the existence of 'tacit knowledge' is that 'we know more than we can tell'. This means that in many instances there can only be induction of one person by another into a practice, rather than instruction. Polanyi discusses this under a number of different aspects, one of which is that our competent performance is often dependent on not paying direct attention to what we are doing. Whenever we do so, we lose our stride and are unable to perform. Since our learning of the skill may itself have been part of an unconscious process, we may never have access to the process by which we learned it. Under these circumstances, our verbal description of what we do may be a confabulation or the recital of what we were ourselves told before we learned the skill, but which had no real role in our learning it.

> We can see this best in the way we possess a skill. If I know how to ride a bicycle or how to swim, this does not mean that I can tell how I manage to keep my balance on a bicycle or keep afloat when swimming. I may not have the slightest idea of how I do this or even an entirely wrong or grossly imperfect idea of it, and yet go on cycling and swimming merrily. Nor can it be said that I know how to bicycle or swim and yet do not know how to co-ordinate the complex pattern of muscular acts by which I do my cycling or swimming. I both know how to carry out these performances as a whole and I also know how to carry out the elementary acts which constitute them,

though I cannot tell what these acts are. This is due to that fact that I am only subsidiarily aware of these things, and our subsidiary awareness of a thing may not suffice to make it identifiable.

(Polanyi 1969, pp. 141–2)

There is another aspect of his theory which has been less widely reported and does not appear to be sufficiently taken into account in the uses of his work made by economic and business writers. Polanyi also suggests that when we learn to use tools to carry out an operation, we simultaneously learn to use them as extensions of our senses, providing us with information about the situation in which we are working, as in the case of a screwdriver providing information about the texture and grain of the material into which the screw is driven and about the quality of the material and form of the screw itself. The tool is integrated into the economy of the perception of the user, whose perceptions of the entire process are mediated by their 'default' perceptions of their own internal states. The screwdriver is not simply a tool but also a sensory probe like the blind person's stick. Polanyi argues that 'interpretative frameworks' are analogous to physical tools in that they come to function as probes through which we become used to processing all information of a particular type. Polanyi's 'tacit knowledge' and 'tacit inference' should therefore not be taken as labels for bodies of mental contents no matter how unconscious. They are also processes and heuristics in which body and mind are tuned and sensitised to generate new knowledge by interaction of body, mind, tools and materials.

Joseph Schumpeter, recent endogenous growth theory and spillover

Equilibrium theories of the market economy describe various mechanisms by which the process of competition results in a convergence of demand and supply. The framework of the economy is taken to be determined by factors external to the economy as a closed system, 'exogenous', such as population growth, new technologies and changes in taste. Among the different Austrian theorists of the alternative view of the market as a dynamic process which has its own internal or 'exogenous' sources of change, the most relevant for our present concern is Schumpeter.[2] His phrase 'waves of creative destruction' summed up the process by which new technologies make possible the creation of new markets for new products which require whole new infrastructures while simultaneously destroying the value of existing infrastructures. By infrastructures we could mean infrastructures of storage and delivery, of wholesale and retail, of maintenance and repair, or of skills and training. Furthermore, the replacement of one dominant technology by another will lead to the use of new materials and methods in many other areas of the economy. In the first centuries of capitalism these waves were spaced out so that the whole economic life of a single individual could pass within a single wave or paradigm. Today we may have to accept that individuals will have to be adjusted to move from one paradigm to another once or several times during their active lives.

Recent endogenous growth theory emphasises the importance of spillover.[3] There are different kinds of spillover. One which may not initially seem to be relevant here is the direct effect of the spillover of income. That is to say, in so far as the entire benefit of any particular innovation is not taken as a rent by the innovator, there is some spillover of income benefit to the wider society within which the innovation takes place. This can be seen by taking the extreme case, in which the innovator can keep the full benefits of the innovation only by paying the prior going rate for all inputs. This assumes that there is no demand pressure on any input, in effect that the economy is in a slump. The normal assumption will be rather that the innovator will need to bid up at least some inputs to divert them from other uses.

The most directly relevant form of spillover discussed in endogenous growth theory is technological spillover. This is the basis of the theories of industrial districts, of clustering and of national competitive advantage. By allowing technological spillover, the innovators accept an initial loss of competitive advantage, but when the process works smoothly, the sharing of technologies will enable firms within a district or cluster to maintain a competitive and innovative advantage over firms outside. Technology sharing and skill sharing mean that firms create pools of skilled labour which can move to the most advantageous new use; that development problems can be rapidly overcome due to availability of experience with equivalent problems; and that firms within the cluster become each other's customers as they require machinery and inter-mediate products to meet expanding order books. Upward pressure on skilled wages is more than compensated by the gains of productivity as technologies and skills are generalised, while the resultant competitive advantage of the cluster as a whole reduces the overall effect of price competition in comparison with design and innovation competition.

A special case of spillover is that associated with Schumpeter's concept of 'creative destruction'. New technologies can lead to the phenomenon of tip-ping, whereby new sources of power or new materials can produce or enable new technologies which sweep the entire economy, introducing new modalities of transportation, storage, preservation and use, making entire infrastructures obsolete and creating new ones. This gives rise to a meta-level of competition between first movers and followers which may go either way. In this case it is an open question whether cost, design or market dynamics will play the major role in the emergence of new standards. But on a national level there is a strong motivation to use technological spillover as a tactic to achieve market share and thus become the standard-setter on a world scale.

Another type of spillover which is of increasing relevance is the spillover of technology from industrial to leisure use or from public to private use. In pre-modern and early modern societies there was spillover from military innovation to industrial use, as instanced by steamships, railways and civil engineering, but this is now very restricted, some argue because military technologies have lost touch with non-military applications. In the twentieth century the telephone, recorded sound, the automobile, the television, the computer and now the mobile phone are the prime instances of the subversion of technologies developed for public or industrial use for private, social and communicative use. We need to think about the effects on skills. The telephone, the automobile, the computer and the mobile phone are all instances of technologies which have a strong crossover effect between private and employment use. There is spillover both ways in that private and employment uses of these technologies can move following different dynamics and one or the other can be the technology leader for periods of time. We are currently experiencing a period in which private computer use appears to be the leader, with governments hoping that household computer use will produce a broadly computer-literate population which will be able to adapt to information-technology-led innovations at work.

At this point, the first kind of spillover does make a difference because access to new technologies is itself a function of income. In societies where there is spillover or crossover between the technologies of leisure and work, income spillover will play a role in increasing skills by increasing familiarity with work-relevant technologies outside of the work application. Of course, in neglecting income spillover we were in any case neglecting the role of education in the production of skills, since education is also correlated with income. But again the spillover or crossover between work technologies and educational technologies will further amplify the effect of income spillover on skills. This was already the case with the automobile and consumer electronics and its relevance for new information and communication technologies is obvious.

The New Economy and innovation diffusion

We suggest that Polanyi's ideas are especially relevant to the necessity for innovation diffusion in the New Economy. We consider that the phrase 'New Economy' is significant as indicating the global nature of the capital market. We do not identify the New Economy with the dot.com phenomenon on the mass market although the New Economy has in fact come about as part of the wider phenomenon of information and communication technology (ICT) development. The New Economy is certainly linked globally by a shuttle of stock, bond, currency and commodity markets which never close in the sense that trading patterns on those closing each day are carried over into those opening at the same time elsewhere. However, for us, the principal reason for identifying the New Economy as a significant departure from what preceded it is not this technical gimmick, but the fact that there is no longer any significant market which is protected from new entrants. This makes innovation the only source of competitive advantage in the long run. Other aspects of the ICT revolution work in the same direction. Despatialisation and outsourcing are currently seen primarily as producing a pull towards sources of cheap labour.

In the longer run they will have the effect of forcing every firm to concentrate on its core business while allowing entrepreneurs to remodel the business markets created by the shedding of non-core activities. This means that entrepreneurial innovation will permeate every activity, revolutionising those which have languished as services within larger organisations.

As the discussion of spillover above will have indicated, we do not adopt the simplistic approach that competitive advantage translates into secrecy about in-house developments. Rather, in the future, competitive advantage will reside primarily in the development of capacity to maintain a dynamic of incremental improvement of products and processes. This requires a number of areas of information exchange. One is the requirement for client feedback, which will have the effect of making the position facing the final client especially attractive and lead to a remodelling of supply and value chains in order to attempt to attain this position. Another is that if all businesses are pressured to concentrate on their core business, they will increasingly be led to develop joint research and development projects with other firms with different competitive advantages. A third is that the position of standard-setter requires wide diffusion of new standards. At the same time, governments are concerned that their populations and business communities are provided with the widest base of generic skills in order to adapt to predictable and unforeseen economic evolution. All of these factors combine to make the rapid diffusion of new skills and competencies something for which there will be an increasing demand. We suggest that the analysis of the tacit component in skill and competency will play multiple roles in any such diffusion processes, which will often have to take place over barriers of professional, sectoral, educational and cultural distance, so that the clear realisation of what implicit and tacit assumptions are made will be essential.

2   The shaping of Michael Polanyi's philosophy

Introduction

In this book we will present the philosophy of Michael Polanyi as we understand it in order to show that his ideas remain important and cannot be reduced to a simple contrast of tacit and explicit knowledge. A fuller understanding of his ideas will throw new light on the entire area of the relationship between skill and knowledge. Although it will not make much sense to most readers at this stage, our conclusion is that the first stage in making Polanyi's ideas more generally useful will consist in mapping the tacit component of all exercises of skill and knowledge. We will not take up the questions of the parallels and convergences of Polanyi with other contemporary or later philosophers. Commentators on Polanyi have suggested common ground with Piaget, Husserl, Merleau-Ponty, Wittgenstein, Dewey and Bentley, and Peirce.[1] Polanyi uses some of the work of Piaget appreciatively, but was probably unaware of the more technically philosophical part of his work, while he was very negative about Wittgenstein, but may have failed to grasp the underlying intentions of his later works. Polanyi (1964b) made a claim that his concept of *indwelling* was equivalent to Heidegger's *being-in-the-world*, but he never returned to this topic.

Leaving aside such questions for later investigation, we will discuss two bodies of philosophical work which directly influenced Polanyi, but which are today relatively unknown. One of these is the gestalt school of Wertheimer, Köhler and Koffka, to which Polanyi makes frequent reference. From the 1940s to the 1960s he stated that his work was a continuation of this approach.[2] The other is that of the overwhelmingly most influential scientist of the physiology of the senses of sight and hearing, Hermann von Helmholtz. Polanyi makes a few references to his theory of unconscious induction as a precursor to his own views on tacit knowing. We will attempt to show that Polanyi's more general ideas of commitment, indwelling and breaking out also owe something to Helmholtz or to his tradition within Central European medical and scientific education. It could be argued that Polanyi was attracted by some aspects of gestalt theory and repelled by others, and that his return to the tradition of

Helmholtz was the result of his search for an alternative. It will also become apparent that while Polanyi certainly wished to argue and indeed prove that positivism ignored great areas of human existence, there remains a significant area of common ground between him and the wider traditions of scientific method which he never repudiated in their proper place. We have therefore decided that the elucidation of Polanyi's ideas will gain much more by reminding readers of the roots of his thinking than by attempting to find parallels and influences among his contemporaries or those who entered the scene after he had begun his independent philosophical explorations. It is also necessary to situate his thought in the political and social context which led to his migration from Germany to England and from the natural to the social sciences and philosophy.

Critical philosophy – making everything explicit

Michael Polanyi subtitled his major work *Personal Knowledge* 'Towards a Post-Critical Philosophy'. The term 'critical philosophy' is technically derived from the philosophy of Kant, but Polanyi wanted to escape from the entire approach of Western philosophy since Descartes, the so-called 'Enlightenment'. He believed that thinkers as various as Descartes, Hobbes, Locke, Leibniz and Kant had all been instrumental in initiating an attempted substitution of a – misunderstood – conception of scientific knowledge for the reality of human experience. The basis of this misconception was an exaggerated emphasis on two strictures which may be valid at some level in philosophical and scientific investigations but which can only be disastrous if they are taken as rules of thumb in everyday life. These were Descartes' proposal to doubt everything and yet to seek perfect knowledge, and Bacon's proposal to generate all possible combinations of factors and treat them all as equally probable.

Ancient societies had known the philosophical school of Scepticism, which doubted everything without offering any escape from doubt. Polanyi sees Descartes as the first of a modern trend which attempt to have their cake and eat it, which he believes led to positivism, Marxism and nihilism. Scepticism was revived by those modern thinkers who wanted to escape from the strife of the wars of religion which followed the Reformation. It was applied to the dogmas of religion and to the theologically underpinned doctrines derived by scholasticism from the philosophy of Aristotle. Polanyi welcomed this as a useful and necessary move towards the freedom of scientific research and the personal quest for truth. But Descartes wanted to use the most extreme scepticism only in order to destroy everything except the one Archimedean point which would allow him to construct a new model of perfect truth. He seeks one indubitable fact which will be the foundation of a new science of everything. The new science which he proposed was that of mechanics, mathematically exact algorithms of the movement of bodies in space.

Positivism – reduction of teleology to dead processes

Positivism was the attempt to turn this programme into reality by 'reducing' all the phenomena of the world to their underlying material basis. The word 'reduction' has a perfectly legitimate use in science. When the principles and contents of two areas of science are found to be congruent, the two sciences are seen to have approached the same object from different sides and they are 'reduced' to a single science, as the sciences of electricity and magnetism became that of 'electromagnetism'. This is a desirable and attainable goal in science. The word 'reductionism' becomes negatively charged when it is implied that the goal is pursued over-hastily or ill-advisedly. In some cases this might arise from the personal vanity or institutional rivalries of scientists. Polanyi thinks that there is a more general problem arising from the fact that the reduction desired in this case can never be achieved, because major elements of the underlying realities are being deliberately ignored. In this case he thinks that to attempt to explain the sciences of living matter as 'reducible' to those of dead matter is a misconceived dogma which as a programme can never be fulfilled but which in the meantime as a prejudice poisons our everyday understanding of the world.

Polanyi accepts that teleology must be excluded from our investigation and understanding of 'dead' nature. He speaks of the fact that non-living nature can never succeed or fail: everything just happens. If a thunderstorm appears to be about to break out, but then doesn't, and the clouds disperse again, we speak metaphorically of a storm which failed to take place, but we do not go on to state positively that the storm failed in its purpose of taking place. A flawed crystal may be less useful to us than a perfect crystal, but the flawed crystal has not intrinsically 'failed' to become a perfect crystal. The study of nature in this sense is legitimately mechanistic. It seeks to explain what actually happens in terms of bodies and forces in space.

Living matter, on the other hand, is characterised by goals. Polanyi argues that we humans instinctively judge living entities in terms of their success or failure in achieving what we take to be their goals. In many cases we may misunderstand the goals of other creatures, but this is in matters of detail. Generally we know what sort of things classes of plants or animals do, and we judge individual members of these species in terms of how well they do these things.

> The moment we identify a plant or an animal we attribute an achievement to it. For we recognise it by its typical shape, which it has achieved by growing up healthily. At the same time we will notice any imperfections of its shape. Thus even when we are considering merely their shapes, we can identify living beings only in terms that attribute success or failure to them as individuals. On this morphological level the centre of individuality is comparatively weak. But the manifestations of this centre become steadily more accentuated as we successively ascend, first, to the vegetative

level of physiological functions, then to active, sentient and appetitive behaviour, thence to the level of intelligence and inventiveness, finally reaching the level of the responsible human person. Each time we identify the existence of an individual at one of these levels we thereby attribute to him a measure of active, responsible intelligence. We know a normal human being as a person, and the particulars of his physiognomy gain a vivid significance by being known in terms of this person.

(Polanyi 1969, p. 135)

Polanyi fully accepted the general outline of the theory of evolution and the emergence of life from non-living matter. But he considered that the materialist explanation of this process lacked something. He was aware of the theories being developed to explain how cells and creatures respond to chemical concentrations and light, but he found these mechanisms inadequate to explain the initial emergence of goal-seeking, particularly in the growth and development of organisms. He was attracted to the idea that on achieving a certain level of complexity, structures of matter began to be susceptible to the effects of force-fields which do not impinge on the processes studied by physics and chemistry. Contemporary science might offer him the more sophisticated alternatives of phase spaces and fitness landscapes, but Polanyi would probably have also found these inadequate. This ultimate longing for some external explanation of life should not detract us from the major thrust of Polanyi's thought, which was to integrate the workings of the mind and body, which he saw as having been torn apart by the acceptance of critical philosophy. Polanyi never made a fetish of any particular suggestion of how life might point beyond itself.

Mechanisms are not machines, and vice versa

Polanyi thought that biologists who attempted to reach the goal of the reduction of biology to physics by the analogy of the machine were totally misguided. He saw machines as externalised embodiments of human intentions. Machines are contraptions whose physical states are wholly determined by the intended purposes for which they are made, while of course constrained by the limitations of the materials used. Finding a strange machine, we can learn how its parts move, but we do not know why it exists unless we know the purpose for which it was made. Generally we can see straight away what a machine is for. This is because we judge a machine as analogous to a living entity, as embodying a teleology which it may achieve more or less well. To attempt to explain living entities on the model of the machine is surreptitiously to import teleology back into the origin of life. Polanyi denied that there were any true machines in non-human nature.

This may seem a digression, but Polanyi was far from seeing human nature in terms of a machine which either does or does not contain a 'ghost'. He saw this as the fundamental problem of the critical philosophy which separated mind from matter. For Polanyi, human beings are living matter which is distinct from dead matter but within which there is no fundamental distinction between mind and matter. It is the whole living body which has goals, feelings, thought, and those higher conceptual faculties specific to the higher animals and man.

Polanyi does not disagree with the project of describing living matter in terms of the 'mechanisms' by which it operates. The problem arises from the false identification of mechanisms with machines. A mechanism is part of something whereas a machine is something self-standing. To say that a biological cell is made up of mechanisms which carry out particular tasks is not the same as saying that it is a machine. Polanyi considers that living matter embodies higher-level laws than non-living matter. Machines also embody these higher-level laws, but only because we have made them so. Their inclusion within these higher-level laws is explained by their origin in our systems of goals and our strategies to attain them. To use these artefacts as a paradigm for systems of matter which are intermediate between non-living and living matter is to reverse the direction of real development and in doing so to obscure the real difficulties of the origin of life.

Science – Baconian dogma belied by intuitive practice

Alongside Descartes, Bacon was mentioned as contributing to the problematic constitution of critical philosophy. This was because of his idea of the pursuit of science without preconceptions. This is actually a good principle, when applied within a restricted field of options, but combined with the principle of universal doubt it gives rise to the practice of considering all conceivable possibilities as of equal prior likelihood. Polanyi thought that modern science paid lip service to this ideal while in reality the progress of scientific research was based on a realistic grasp of the possibility of certain avenues of research being likely to be fruitful. In fact the dogma of preconception-less research was much less dangerous in the laboratory than in its extension to everyday life, where it contributed to undermining commonsense appreciation of reality. But it also continually reappeared in the philosophy of science, giving rise to a dichotomy of scientific theory and practice which misled the lay public about the reality of scientific work.

Polanyi's own theory of scientific method was that while science requires that there should be rigorous experimental conditions, statistically significant testing, and a process of thorough peer review of all results, the initial choice of what experiments to carry out was part of the process of tacit knowing and the personal commitment of scientists. There could never be an exhaustive testing of all possible alternatives, nor a rigorous method for selecting the most likely avenues of advance. Hypotheses necessarily arise from the personal knowledge of experienced scientists who are aware of both the generally accepted paradigm of their field and the areas of growth and development. As in the more general field of the application of tacit knowing, the most important thing is to know what not to do and what outcomes are impossible. This does not mean that the ruling assumptions of the scientific community are always right, but they are the only way for science to advance systematically. A complete openness to every conceivable possibility can never become a practical programme for testing every possibility in reality.

Nihilism – dichotomy of fact and values

The practice of positivist science in the nineteenth century gave rise to a general understanding that facts and values were different universes. This effectively 'devalued' values altogether, since positivism denied validity to any source of truth except mechanistic science. But a world which denies the applicability of values itself becomes valueless, and in this way the whole world became something which, since we probably cannot genuinely be value-free, became negative. Nihilism as portrayed in Turgenev's character Bazarov responds by a fierce commitment to science as the only value. The answer proposed by Nietzsche was that we need to set new values. His approach was a mirror image of the Cartesian project of finding an Archimedean point to change the world.

Polanyi grew up in a society where most educated young people were subjected to the choices of Bazarov or Nietzsche: either science was the only value or else completely new values must be found from some prophetic source. In either case, traditional values were seen as false and self-contradictory. In Polanyi's view this leads to a deep crisis for society because in reality human beings cannot separate facts and values, which are inextricably linked in all of our thoughts and actions. The predominant solution to this was Marxism.

Marxism – combination of value-free science and moral outrage

Polanyi makes it clear that he is talking about the popular Marxism of his own time, which he diagnoses as a continuation of the dynamic and dilemmas of positivism. This popular Marxism, in his view, rescued the values of existing society by projecting their realisation into the indefinite future, while condemning values as a means of achieving that future, which instead was to be the work of science alone. All of the energy which was generated by the discrepancy between the values of liberal society and the reality of semi-feudal Central Europe was given the refuge of a crypto-scientific expression in scientific socialism. Not only all contemporary values but the very idea of value itself could be dispensed with by adherence to a 'purely' scientific creed of social change. The Marxist movement competed with and shaded off into other forms of progressivism which embodied the same mechanism but became the predominant form of the syndrome in the twentieth century.

While Polanyi is a liberal, he does not primarily criticise Marxism for its analysis or its programme, but because it served as a channel for the psychic problems which arose from the background of positivism. The programme of doubting all knowledge, of accepting only indubitable facts as valid knowledge, of equating these with mechanistic explanations, and of seeking to make all knowledge scientific and of banishing all other forms of discourse, created the nihilistic dichotomy of a factual valueless world and an alienated mind in search of values. The classes affected by this process created Marxism as a mass movement expressing their moral outrage in the language of value-free science.[3]

On the basis of this background, it is possible to investigate Polanyi's theory of knowledge on the understanding that his aim is to reverse the processes which he associates with the rise of critical philosophy. He will argue that facts and values, body and mind, knowledge and action, persons and contexts, are in each case inseparable. He will argue that the emphasis on knowledge itself within critical philosophy is pernicious and should be exchanged for a centrality of human goal-driven action in the world which overcomes even the – for him central – dichotomy of the living and the non-living, because our goals and actions are ultimately derived from the interactions between the living and the non-living.

Polanyi is impatient with the traditional philosophical problem of 'other minds' since he sees this as a consequence of the 'ghost in the machine' assumption, which he rejects. We know that other people are like us because we are human beings who know that we are bodies. We know that other people are like us and that they also share our experiences of light, sound, smell, taste and touch, although in some people these senses are obviously deficient or biased in some ways. We likewise know that other people have goals and intentions like us and expectations like us. We cannot help knowing this, and we cannot help judging other people – and other creatures – on this basis. Indeed, we are likely to over-generalise and to apply these criteria to a wider range of humans and creatures than is truly appropriate. But this is the basis from which we start and on which we build up whatever more nuanced understandings we may be able to develop. We cannot get 'behind' this starting point.

Polanyi in England

In his essay 'Beyond Nihilism' (1960)[4] Polanyi described the social world of his own youth in Hungary in the wider context of the social and intellectual movements affecting Central and Eastern Europe in the early decades of the twentieth century, in which he played a personal part and was connected with the most influential circles through his brother, the sociologist and political activist Karl Polanyi. In the 1920s he dedicated himself to his career as a chemist and crystallographer, leading to his becoming a life member of the Kaiser Wilhelm Gesellschaft with a research laboratory in Berlin. In 1933 Polanyi took up a position in Manchester for which he had been negotiating before Hitler's accession to power. He was a Jew by birth, although a Christian by personal belief, but his employment would have been protected for some time by his having served in the Great War. However, he was convinced that the Hitler regime would not become more moderate, as many still hoped at that time. In England he became convinced that a simplistic understanding of science played a great part in the expectations which many on the left had of economic and social planning. Through his friendships with Karl Mannheim, Friedrich von Hayek and Arthur Koestler, among others, he became involved in circles which believed that the reassertion of liberal values against totalitarian systems of the left and right required a more realistic understanding of the nature of science as an open-ended process of continual discovery and debate. He was strengthened in this by a meeting in 1935 with Bukharin in Moscow, in which the latter argued strongly for the subordination of scientific research to the needs of the Five Year Plan. This is the background against which Polanyi began to develop his ideas of personal knowledge in the 1940s.[5]

3 Michael Polanyi's theory of personal knowledge

Tacit knowing – most knowledge has to be backgrounded

Polanyi begins from the fact that the greatest part of our knowledge is sub-servient to our goals and actions. It is in the background but is not called on in the form of statements. Most of what we do is done on the basis of routines which are familiar and within which we follow established patterns and fami-liar heuristics of interpretation of what is taking place. We cannot focus on the knowledge necessary to accomplish these actions without detracting from the performance itself, and so risking 'putting ourselves off'. In extreme cases, such as repetitively operating a very simple machine, we can 'switch off' completely. When we have to concentrate on a skilled action we are mostly focusing on what could go wrong rather than on the positive components, which are necessary but which can be taken for granted.

This is tacit knowing, but what is tacit knowledge? If we looked at our knowledge from the point of view of logical implication, our knowledge could be said to be infinite. Linguistics tells us that we can generate an infinite number of sentences. Does that mean that we 'know' how to do this? Knowledge of classes of things can likewise generate infinite knowledge of the individuals of these classes and their parts and their possible interaction with other things. In Polanyi's way of thinking there is no ultimate distinction between 'knowing that' and 'knowing how'. Knowing how to carry out a skilled performance of any action includes having the capacity to generate a potentially infinite stock of judgements about the progress of the action and the possible risks of failure.

Focal and subsidiary awareness

The section of *Personal Knowledge* entitled 'Two Kinds of Awareness' introduces what is probably the central component of Polanyi's theory: the distinction of *focal awareness* and *subsidiary awareness*. The most innovative idea expressed here is that 'When we bring down the hammer we do not feel that its handle has struck our palm but that its head has struck the nail' (1958, p. 55). The example of the hammer is followed by that of the blind man's stick, or of a probe used to investigate a cavity (1958, pp. 54–5). In each of these cases we have an awareness of what is at the end of the tool, which is achieved by integrating the feelings in our hand and fingers to model what is happening outside our body, at a location which we may or may not also be able to see. Beginners look at the hammer, but experienced users can feel whether the head of the hammer is moving in the right way to drive in the nail. For experienced users, looking at the hammer is actually distracting, and 'puts us off' in the same way as does thinking about playing the piano while playing. *Focal awareness* is the awareness of our purpose, while all of the particulars of how to achieve this have to become submerged in our *subsidiary awareness* in order for the action to be successful. Polanyi suggests that this is because 'our attention can hold only one focus at a time and that it would hence be self-contradictory to be both subsidiarily and focally aware of the same particulars at the same time' (1958, p. 57).[1]

Hammering in a nail and riding a bicycle are activities which have been identified as peculiar to human beings:

Lorenz suggests that no animal below man is capable of driving a nail straight into a piece of wood. Such an action is certainly not an ultimate test of intelligence and would perhaps not be suspected of having anything to do with intelligence until one realizes that it is not because of lack of strength, of inability to hold or swing a hammer, or of lack of interest, that primates as well as young children, cannot perform this task. What is lacking are the rules of coordination that govern the strokes which compensate for each slight deviation from the vertical. Lower organisms do not have the capacity for this elementary degree of learned skill which can be called 'control of an action pattern by continuous compensatory movements'. Intelligence is found thus, not in the activity as such, but in the rule which implicitly governs this activity.

(Furth 1969, p. 151)

One of the few attempts to theorise about the connections between human attention and action provides a possible explanation:

attentional control is probably too slow and unwieldy to provide the high precision of accuracy and timing needed to perform skilled acts. Deliberate conscious control is generally agreed to involve serial processing steps, each step taking on the order of 100 msec. or more. Such control would simply be too slow to account for skilled human behaviour that requires action sequences to be initiated just when environmental or internal conditions call for them; in some situations they must be accurate to the nearest 20 msec. This is consistent with the general view that deliberate control of skilled performance leads to deterioration of performance.

(Norman and Shallice 1986/2000, pp. 384–5)

This may be understood in the context of human plasticity. Animals are perhaps capable of executing and switching between instinctual behaviour patterns at speeds equivalent to those cited, but they have no capacity to switch attention and therefore action between learned behaviours at the same speeds. This is because they are not built for learning a wide range of new behaviours. It would follow that animals would not have developed the additional pathways which must allow the summation of input relevant to particular sub-contexts of action which we must suppose are the basis of human tacit skill.[2]

Polanyi's collaborator Marjorie Grene found that Polanyi was intent on maintaining the distinction between two types of awareness, the focal and the subsidiary, to such an extent that he was resistant to accepting a third category of components in the process to accommodate those elements of which we are not aware at all. Reporting a conversation she participated in, she states:

> Am I aware of the neurons firing in my brain as I write this? They are subsidiary to the focus of my attention: I rely on them in order to accomplish my task. But surely, I am not aware of them at all. [Hubert] Dreyfus had a long discussion with Polanyi, probably about 1969, in which he argued that it was quite inappropriate to speak of 'awareness' in this context: it is the integral bearing of the subsidiary on the organization of the focal that matters, whether we can be aware of it or not. Thus subsidiaries may lie, and often do, beyond the range of awareness altogether. Polanyi was adamant: it was two kinds of awareness he had started from and would stick to, the kind of awareness exemplified in the learning and practice of skills. Yet the 'from' of the from–to relation does seem to vary from any degree of awareness to none at all.
>
> (Grene 1977, p. 170)

This problem is of great practical importance for the project of mapping the tacit component of knowledge and skills. Yet it seems that there are grounds for taking both sides in relation to different aspects of the problem. From the point of view of a philosophical understanding, it must be the case that for Polanyi it can be said that we draw on our entire body in focusing on any process outside ourselves, since the tokens of what is outside us have arisen and become organised within us on the basis of a particular attunement of our whole body and are brought into activation by a similar whole-body activity. On the other hand, the dynamic of focal and subsidiary awareness seems to require paying special attention to how different elements of our knowledge and bodily preparedness are activated and deactivated, foregrounded and backgrounded, in different closely succeeding phases of a single process. From this point of view the involvement of those processes which never attain awareness is perhaps of little operational relevance under normal circumstances and would not become part of the mapping unless there were a special reason to suppose that they do in fact become significantly more active or dormant in different phases.

The from–to relationship

Our knowing is always part of a process of achieving something. The objects we use are also part of processes which proceed to a goal. Polanyi uses the term 'from–to relationship' to emphasise how our actions and tools are goal-determined.

He considers that there are two stages in the tacitness of knowledge. When we are engaged in any action we focus on the aim and we background all of the conditions of success of the action unless and until they become a problem. But we also focus through the object of our action on the ultimate aim for which the action is undertaken. Our judgement of whether the action is proceeding adequately is not generally determined by a fixed idea of what the physical form of the outcome should be but by whether it is an adequate basis for the next stage of a continuous chain of actions. This can be seen in terms of making things, walking, carrying on a conversation, or more complicated processes in science, social affairs, war or art. In modern society we have become accustomed to see action through the paradigm of the manufacture of a series of almost identical and for all practical purposes interchangeable objects. This is a misleading paradigm for the teleology of most human action, which is driven not by approximation to a blueprint but by adequacy to a goal. This final goal is itself not a blueprint but is subject to shifting conceptions of what success would consist of and how to achieve it.

Articulation

The section of *Personal Knowledge* entitled 'Articulation' contains a series of approaches to the question of the role of the tacit component in the emergence of articulate, that is to say explicit or codified, knowledge. This is important for the unravelling of the false problematic of 'making tacit knowledge explicit'. Polanyi is not positing the existence of a source of knowledge unknown to anyone previous to him. He is rather arguing that Cartesianism and positivism have devalued most of the real knowledge of humanity by reserving the word 'knowledge' for those propositions which are adjudged by actual or only postulated authorities to conform to conditions of validity derived from Plato's discussions of 'episteme'. Whereas Descartes thought that it was possible to find a bedrock of 'certain' knowledge, more recent positivism has been satisfied with a more restricted, probable and fallible form of knowledge, but most of the knowledge really in existence still does not meet the criteria of positivist science. Polanyi argues that the results of real active scientific investigation also do not meet the criteria of positivism, and that the search for a touchstone of truth prior to knowledge of real things and real processes is a chimera.

Against this background, most of our explicit and codified knowledge becomes questionable. First, most of codified knowledge is not really used in everyday life. Second, because explicit knowledge is generally prescriptive and based on a mixture of descriptions which may be outmoded and supposedly basic principles which may actually be invalid and which also may be out of fashion in theory, it is not easy to apply because it is out of touch both with the reality it supposedly describes and with the actual presuppositions of the individuals concerned. Third, the retrieval, use and interpretation of codified knowledge are themselves processes, the success of which depends on the mobilisation of a range of tacit components of their own.

Marjorie Grene, at one point a researcher working for Polanyi during the preparation of *Personal Knowledge*, states:

> I did not really understand at the time why just this problem, the grounding of the articulate in the inarticulate, should need to be spelled out so painfully. But it is indeed the heart of the matter – not, again, because Polanyi was developing an 'irrationalism' (a 'neo-obscurantism', as one reviewer called it), but because the understanding of understanding, of rationality itself, demands an understanding of the way in which the subsidiary supports the focal, in particular of the way in which the ineffable supports the activities of voice or pen.
>
> (Grene 1977, p. 168)

Polanyi announced that he would begin his approach to the question of articulation by examination of three 'characteristic areas in which the relation between speech and thought varies from one extreme type to an opposite extreme, through the intermediary of a balanced type', namely:

> (1) The area where the tacit predominates to the extent that articulation is virtually impossible; we may call this the *ineffable domain*. (2) The area where the tacit component is the information conveyed by easily intelligible speech, so that *the tacit is co-extensive with the text of which it carries the meaning*. (3) The area in which the tacit and the formal fall apart, since the speaker does not know, or quite know, what he is talking about. There are two extremely different cases of this, namely (a) an ineptitude of speech, owing to which articulation encumbers the tacit work of thought; (b) symbolic operations that outrun our understanding and thus anticipate novel modes of thought.
>
> (Polanyi 1958, p. 87)

Polanyi's example of the *ineffable domain* is something which he believes is not merely unexpressed, but the expression of which is inconceivable except through the actual use of the skill to which it gives rise, namely the ability of a surgeon to gestalt the three-dimensional interconnections of a body on which they are operating. The information involved is itself completely articulable, but it can be explicitly expressed and absorbed only through the media of speech or diagrams, both of which impose a loss through their inherent directionality (speech) or dimensional loss (diagrams). Three-dimensional models and film of actual operations have the same inherent directionality; that is to say, one can only dismantle so much of a multi-layered model without losing the feel of the whole, and film is no different from speech in being spread out through time. The individual's ability to map the route they will follow through tissue which is not yet opened up is something which is different from any possible description, representation or modelling of it, at least in the sense that no articulation of it will ever present to the mind all of the information which the mind gestalts instantaneously and simultaneously (Polanyi 1958, p. 89).

Polanyi does not merely wish to say that this kind of knowledge cannot be conveyed without loss of detail. It would be equally true to say that when we describe a route from one place in our town we must necessarily leave out a lot of detail. But we can imagine or construct in a computer a maze which has no features to be lost, and consists only of the turnings, yet the gestalt of a three-dimensional maze is an experience which we cannot express through a map or a verbal description, since the simultaneity of the aspects is necessarily absent. Our means of communication are simply inadequate to convey the actual experience of knowing how a body, an engine or any other complex system is actually working and how to intervene in it, even though large amounts of the components of this experience can be communicated. Polanyi illustrates this problem with a medical example, but he also struggled with this problem when trying to develop graphic means for conveying the complexity of the economy.[3]

Polanyi's second point is even more difficult to grasp until we have absorbed some understanding of his general theory. Words and grammatical structures have standard meanings, and the 'meaning' of a sentence is made up of these. However, Polanyi does not think that most 'explicit' or 'codified' communication genuinely consists of a simple transfer of information from the sender to the receiver. Rather, every understanding of an utterance is an interpretation, and every interpretation is informed by the active concern of the receiver with the matter in hand. This is not simply a question of the fact that every act of understanding consists of a mass of implicit and tacit operations in decoding the message and ascribing it to a particular context, important though these tacit elements are. Beyond this, Polanyi considers that every understanding of the words of others is already an active part of our own active grasping of the meaning of the world. We never simply 'understand' what others are saying without integrating it into our complete dynamic grasp of the world. In his terms, every statement we hear or letter we read is something to which we subsidiarily attend while focally our attention is already moving beyond the bare bones of the communication towards its meaning *as we see it* in the context of our own concerns and expectations. Within the context of indwelling this will also mean that we will integrate the tacit expectations and concerns of others *as we see them* in constructing our interpretation. While we all feel that we can put ourselves in the other's place and see the other side of situations as they see them to a certain extent, we are unaware of how much of our own concerns goes into the interpretation of all ostensibly 'explicit' communication. This is why real 'hermeneutic', the secondary indwelling which Polanyi found at work in Dilthey's practice of reliving, is a recent phenomenon. It is difficult to go beyond the simple adoption of the other's material standpoint, seeing problems from the point of view of their needs and interests, to seeing that words themselves cannot be taken as having a common meaning separate from the different integrations of lived experience which are 'expressed' in them.

Polanyi concludes his discussion of this point by reminding us that 'While focal awareness is necessarily conscious, subsidiary awareness may vary over all degrees of consciousness' (1958, p. 92). He suggests that we can have a completely conscious but nevertheless deeply subsidiary awareness of the words we are hearing or reading, while simultaneously our real focal awareness is on the import of the message as we see it within the pattern of our concerns and other background knowledge.

Polanyi's third point takes up the process of articulating the tacit. He begins by referring to the work of Piaget, who demonstrated that children have to learn all over again to carry out by explicit means processes which they have already mastered tacitly or implicitly, to which we could now set in parallel the work of Lave on adults and older children who have never learned the explicit counterpart to their tacit skills.[4] He then discusses the problems of false belief arising from attempts at the formalisation of knowledge. Magic and superstition are universal wherever they have not been overcome by science, but science itself has developed systems of formal operations and symbolisation which had existed for thousands of years before faults were discovered in their basic assumptions. Language and other symbolisations of explicit thought are open to over-generalisation and the generation of error. The systematic formalisation of knowledge can also generate new knowledge, or can produce resources the full potential of which may never be realised, as 'We may recall as a crude model of this how even a small map multiplies a thousand-fold the original input of information; and add to this that, actually, the number of meaningful and interesting questions one could study by means of such a map is much greater and not wholly foreseeable' (Polanyi 1958, p. 94).

In the work of Ikujiro Nonaka and his associates, the process of articulation has been taken as the cornerstone of an ambitious project of the 'conversion' of tacit knowledge into explicit knowledge.[5] This is a real process, but it is part of a continuum along which different areas of personal knowledge are more or less difficult to articulate. In reaction to the global circulation of knowledge projected by Nonaka, Boisot (1998, p. 57) proposed a more modest trichotomy of explication of tacit knowledge, namely:

1   Things which everyone takes for granted and which are therefore never made explicit until the organisation encounters outsiders who do not share their assumptions.

2 Things which are only dimly understood as part of a practice or experience within a context; these things cannot be fully made explicit, outsiders can be inducted but not instructed.
3 Things which can be made explicit and formalised, but at a cost. This is both a resource cost, of time and effort, and a cost of loss of concreteness.

This is valid as far as it goes, but our argument suggests that this approach overlooks the tacit component in all uses of skill and knowledge, both those which are apparently arcane and difficult and those which are ubiquitous and well documented. It also leads to seeing 'tacit knowledge' as a problem of management needing to understand the craft secrets of workers, whereas the real problem is that in many areas no one knows how skills and knowledge are evolving in the dynamic use of new technologies. The identification and mapping of new skills and of their tacit component are essential to the best use of new technologies by society as a whole and also have a health-and-safety aspect. We need procedures for investigating new skills which use the degree to which they can be articulated as one factor among others in mapping the process of diffusion.

Commitment – most values have to be unquestioned

Polanyi uses the word 'commitment' to signify the fact that in order to doubt any particular thing meaningfully, we must make prior commitments to the validity of a wide range of other things.[6] His understanding is drawn from scientific and medical practice but he considers that it has general applicability. We can never ourselves question and investigate the vast range of assumptions on which our lives are based. We must accept the traditions into which we are born, educated and inducted in order to be able to add to them or expand them. Otherwise we have no language in common with others. Most individuals do not set out to question the accepted assumptions but to achieve their aims within these shared sets of values. Scientists are specialists in questioning and changing our basic parameters but most scientists are lay persons outside their own field.

Polanyi is not arguing for social stability and conservatism as such. He is aware that the problem with radical thinking is not that it really questions the values of society but that it wishes and claims to do so without having any real grasp of the scope of the problem. He argues that the dialectic of nihilism and Marxism has occurred precisely because people have been persuaded of the one central dogma of positivism, the limitation of valid knowledge to mechanistic algorithms, but that far from putting this into practice they continue to think and act morally as before but without access to a language of morality. This precludes them from developing or reforming morality in accordance with new social developments more effectively than adherence to any conservative dogma could.

So the proposal that we should accept that most values cannot be challenged is an argument not that we should desist from challenging values, but that we should abandon the illusion that we are actually doing so when in reality we are not. In everyday life this means that when we enter into an occupation or any social sphere, we are committing ourselves to absorbing most of the values of that way of life as our background defaults which allow us to distinguish normal from unusual situations and unproblematic from problematic encounters and processes. We can question whether things are done in the right way but first we must know how they are done. And precisely this information is not reliably transmitted by explicit verbal statements but can only be absorbed in practice. It has layers which become apparent only once one has penetrated previous layers, which actually means allowing ourselves to accept the norms of the context whether we wish to or not.

More fundamentally, the underlying idea is that the modern emphasis on the status of knowledge has led us to forget the importance of trust. When we walk into a room and sit on a chair we do not suppose that the floor or the chair will collapse under us. Polanyi considers that the assumption of modern science, that this trust is based on knowledge or belief, is simply false. Trust, reliance, is an evolutionarily primary factor by virtue of which we take our perceptions as reality and our expectations as unquestioned. Analysis of the status of knowledge and belief is a very recent cultural artefact and plays no role in what we all do most of the time in everyday life. It is a mistake to import these notions into any attempted scientific explanation of perception and behaviour.

Polanyi argues that we cannot actually live without trust, and that giving up one commitment only really occurs when another one can take its place. This has important implications for social capital and for the social and economic phenomenon of tipping, in so far as we do not evaluate environments in fine statistical terms, but simply as safe or unsafe, with drastic consequences of altered behaviour when we are forced to alter our evaluations.

Indwelling – experience must be part of a context which we accept as our context

There is a further stage of commitment, which is indwelling.[7] Indwelling means accepting a particular context as a context which defines us and will continue to be involved with us. Polanyi is a liberal and in a sense an individualist but he does not start from the assumption of a straightforward boundary between the individual and their environment, any more than of one between mind and body. The development of our goals and aims, and the habits and heuristics which we need to achieve them, means becoming embedded in and determined by the contexts which we choose. The nature of tacit knowledge as a bank of values for parameters which are relevant in some contexts and not others means that we can develop our powers and aptitudes only in adjustment to particular contexts. But these contexts are not themselves neutral environments. Because they are human creations, they embody human teleologies and in becoming part of them we absorb the aims and goals of our context as well as the bald data of how things are done. Human beings – and other living creatures – are the centres from which goal-directed action radiates, but the process of achieving goals is also a process of formation in which the understanding of how to achieve goals can become involved in a process of redefining goals and of what would or would not count as achieving them.

Personal knowledge

We have a fund of knowledge about objects and processes which is embedded in our commitment to values, contexts and goals. Personal knowledge is thus a process of continual development and discovery which is also a continual process of adjustment of the individual to their contexts. In principle this kind of knowledge is perspectivist, in that the precise outcome is unique to the situation and history of every individual, but this does not take place on the basis of the disinterested observation of the universe by encapsulated individuals. Every perspective is the centre of a network rather than a naked Archimedean point or an isolated monad. Our adjustment to the regularities and expectations of our contexts is inextricably linked with adoption of goals and redefinition of our goals by these same contexts. Apprenticeship and induction provide structured environments which standardise the process for the majority of individuals who enter them. Learning-by-watching can function as an effective means of induction where the environment contributes to guide the action. Learning-by-doing can itself function as an induction into established practices where the material, tools and expected outcomes contribute to mould the behaviour of the learner. Explicit instruction may be a poor substitute for such induction, particularly when the material framework of processes, materials and tools is itself in flux.

Physiognomy

One of the new features of Polanyi's *The Tacit Dimension* (1966) was a discussion of the work on 'subception' of Lazarus and McCleary, and Eriksen and Kuethe,[8] which can be seen as precursors of the implicit learning approach of Arthur Reber. Whereas Reber and other implicit learning experimenters use reward systems to motivate their subjects to select or reject items from an array, these earlier workers used electric shocks to condition subjects to react to items in a range, the specific characteristics of which were never made explicit. In the first set of experiments, the subjects eventually showed signs of anticipation of the shock whenever the portentous items were displayed, while in the second set, in which the shocks were triggered by a response to the 'shock syllables', subjects began to avoid responding to these particular syllables. In both cases the subjects were unable to explain how they were able to identify the 'shock syllables', and they remained unaware of the specificity of their own reactions to the triggers. Polanyi (1966, p. 9) proposed an explanation of these phenomena in terms of his theory as follows: 'Why did this connection remain tacit? It would seem that this was due to the fact that the subject was riveting his attention on the electric shock. He was relying on his awareness of the shock-producing particulars only in their bearing on the electric shock.'

Polanyi strangely does not seem to confront the design of the tests, which were intended to make it impossible for the subjects to become consciously aware of the specificity of the 'shock syllables'. His will to present the tests as evidence for his theory of the two types of awareness, focal and subsidiary, seems to have overcome the attraction of alternative explanations which could have been equally compatible with his ideas.

He proceeds to do the same thing with facial recognition: 'We are attending *from* the features *to* the face, and thus may be unable to specify the features' (Polanyi 1966, p. 10). Polanyi does not seem to recognise a need to defend the idea that we could be able to specify the features explicitly, but proceeds directly to suggest an explanation of why we do not actually do this. Although the path of his reasoning is not very clear over the next few pages, his conclusion is worth serious consideration:

> We could say . . . that a characteristic physiognomy is the meaning of its features; which is, in fact, what we do say when a physiognomy expresses a particular mood. To identify a physiognomy would then amount to relying on our awareness of its features for attending to their joint meaning. This may sound far-fetched, because the meaning of the features is observed at the same spot where the features are situated, and hence it is difficult to separate mentally the features from their meaning. Yet, the fact remains that the two are distinct, since we may know a physiognomy without being able to specify its particulars.
>
> (Polanyi 1966, p. 12)

One way of reading this would be very significant for both face recognition and other diagnostic systems which may use the same mechanism. This would be as follows:

1   we first recognise a face as a face by virtue of the presence of some face-like features;
2   we then begin to interpret the face as a face;
3   we rapidly map the specific features of the face;
4   we are then able to interpret the mood of the person by subtracting from the sum of the features those which we know to be characteristic for that person;
5   we have developed the ability to do this because the mood the person is in is the most important fact we need to know about them;

6 the high development of our ability to distinguish and identify individuals is a by-product of our need to diagnose the mood that others are in.

This makes sense since humans living in small groups would never need to identify a single individual from thousands or millions of others. It would be fascinating if our ability to recognise faces actually arises from the need to be able to abstract from them to an underlying reality of social interaction. This would also have implications for the possible secondary uses of facial recognition processes in recognising other complex patterns.

Polanyi's approach can also be relevant to the modern concept of *confabulation*. Contemporary brain science proposes that much of the 'wallpaper' of our world is generated by the brain, which takes snapshots of our environment and confabulates a tissue of interconnecting fillers that saturate the boundaries which we perceive on different channels and which we also extrapolate into connected systems of edges. The question of how fine-grained this process is would be a test case for the theory of tacit knowing. Polanyi was very interested in the process of learning how to interpret X-rays, pathology slides, stereoscopies and similar artefactual diagnostic aids, and also the similar process of interpretation of rock striations. He discussed the process by which students are inducted into these skills by a combination of explicit learning of background information about what might be going on inside a lung or a crystal, combined with a continuous process of trial and error in judging exemplars, whether in reality or from primers produced for this purpose.

The messy gradations of a pulmonary X-ray or a pathology slide are instances where the lay person or novice would confabulate continuities because of a lack of attention combined with the natural perceptual mechanism which fills in gaps in input. Contrary to a perhaps caricatured version of associationism, the lay person would not be seeing the evidence but ignoring it through ignorance of its significance, but rather would not see it at all. This is an insight which could lead to a method for the scientific investigation of the reality of tacit knowing, since the unconscious inferences of trained and untrained individuals ought to produce different results in their reports of what they see.

Probes and heuristics

The tools which we use, both physical and mental, become extensions of our body. In the case of tools, we adjust our propriosensory settings so that we process the information received as being 'out there', as we do with sight and hearing input. In the case of heuristics we also make the reality of their postulates part of our world, like assuming the solidity of floors and chairs, and we experience an equivalent shock when they are invalidated. This is another part of commitment, which arises because we cannot constantly check all parameters and values. We must take some things for granted in order to be able to apply ourselves to action.

The process of reliance on a probe which Polanyi calls *projection* was described by Huxley (1895/6) under the designation *extradition*. Huxley does not make any positive use of the phenomenon, but utilises it only in a counter-factual argument about the locality of the mind in reference to the arguments of Bishop Berkeley.

Huxley, 'Hume', 1896	Polanyi, 1969
It has been seen that when the finger is pricked with a pin, a state of consciousness arises which we call pain . . . we know that the feeling of pain caused by the prick of the pin is dependent on the integrity of those fibres (which connect the finger to the brain). After they have been cut through . . . no pain will be felt, whatever injury is done to the finger; and if the ends which remain in connection with the spinal cord be pricked, the pain which arises will appear to have its seat in the finger just as distinctly as before. It is perfectly obvious, therefore, that the localisation of the pain at the surface of the body is an act of the mind. It is an *extradition* of that consciousness, which has its seat in the brain, to a definite point of the body – which takes place without our volition, and may give rise to ideas which are contrary to fact . . . The tactile sensation is referred outwards to the point touched, and seems to exist there. But it is certain that it is not and cannot be there really, because the brain is the sole seat of consciousness; and, further, because evidence, as strong as that in favour of the sensation being in the finger, can be brought forward in support of propositions which are manifestly absurd. For example, the hairs and nails are utterly devoid	A similar projection takes place in the use of tools and probes, and the process can be studied here more easily, since the stimuli that are projected here can be fairly well observed in themselves. The relevant facts are well known. The rower pulling an oar feels the resistance of the water; when using a paper-knife we feel the blade cutting the pages. The actual impact of the tool on our palm and fingers is unspecifiable in the same sense in which the muscular acts composing a skilful performance are unspecifiable; we are aware of them in terms of the tool's action on its object, that is, in the comprehensive entity into which we integrate them. But the impacts of a tool on our hands are integrated in a way similar to that by which internal stimuli are integrated to form our perceptions: the integrated stimuli are noticed at a distance removed outward from the point where they impinge on us. In this sense impacts of a tool on our hands function as internal stimuli, and a tool functions accordingly as an extension of our hands. The same is true of a probe used for exploring a cavity, or for a stick by which a blind man feels his way. The impact made by a probe or stick on our fingers is felt at the tip of the probe or stick, where it hits on objects outside, and in this sense the probe or stick is an extension

of sensibility, as everyone knows. Nevertheless if the ends of the nails and hair are touched, ever so lightly, we feel that they are touched, and the sensation seems to be situated in the nails or hairs. Nay more, if a walking-stick, a yard long, is held firmly by the handle and the other end is touched, the tactile sensation, which is a state of our own consciousness, is unhesitatingly referred to the end of the stick, and yet no one will say that it is there. (Cited by Burtt 1932, pp. 312–14)	of our fingers that grasp it. The assimilation of a tool, a stick or a probe to our body is achieved gradually, as its proper use is being learned and perfected. The more fully we master the use of the instrument, the more precisely and discriminatingly will we localize at the farther end of it stimuli impinging on our body while grasping and handling the instrument. This corresponds to the way we learn skilfully to use our eyes to see external objects. (Polanyi 1969, pp. 127–8)

Very early experiments with up–down and left–right reversing spectacles and mirrors, and with angularity adjustments, showed that after a period of weeks the subjective experience of vision snaps back into place as the visual input is securely mapped onto propriocentric spatial data and external objects; that is to say, our internal feelings of up and down and verticality are derived from our senses of balance and posture and from the feel of the drag of gravity on our bodies and on objects we manipulate, and eventually visual data which contradicts the evidence of the other senses is realigned or remapped to concord with consensus of their data.[9]

The information from probes, the blind person's stick, the rower's oar, the carpenter's screwdriver, the punter's pole or a bent probe used to investigate an inaccessible recess is not experienced as an event in or on the user's hand and fingers but as data about what is really there in the appropriate part of space mapped relative to the person's whole body and external object space. This is not surprising as we also locate our own hand not solely by information from the hand but from the entire arm and body. We learn to interpret the messages from our nerves as being 'about' our hands and fingers only by patterns of correlation between visual and kinetic information of grasping and manipulating objects. Our sensations of exactly where on our back a sensation has occurred are much less exact because most of us do not practise this. We can therefore learn to interpret a particular pattern of pressures on our fingertips as being 'about' something six inches away or a pattern of pressures on the palms of our hands being 'about' something six feet away. In these cases we do not constantly perform physical calculations about the pressure on our nerves and the resistance encountered at such-and-such a distance. We have simply become accustomed to associate this pattern with the feel of the screw encountering hard, soft or rotten wood, or the pole encountering stone, clay or soft mud.

Polanyi considers that our heuristics work in the same way. We have expectations about the likely future actions of rocks and chairs, trees and animals. We each have a differently tuned set of these expectations based on our experience of these things. This affects both the expectations we have and the way in which we classify things into classes with different expectations. The heuristics of higher-level skills are similar and presumably use the same mechanism. Such heuristics are an extension of the self into the world in the same way as physical probes. We experience the same feelings of shock and harm when our most familiar heuristics do not 'work' as when we sit on a chair and it collapses. Our reasonable and normally reliable map of the world and our place and potential for action within it are suddenly upset.

Breaking out and turning around

Bertrand Russell regards knowledge by acquaintance as referring only to knowledge of sense-data, because identifying these sense-data as being a table, a man or a stone requires the application of general ideas (Russell 1998, pp. 25–32). Helmholtz and gestalt theory assert that there is no normal experience of sense-data alone but that we cannot help seeing real things. Helmholtz described this as the 'unconscious induction', an evolutionary adjustment to pragmatic needs, namely the need to operate with real entities, while the gestaltists developed their theories of the perceptual field generated by spatial configurations, the passive-receptive aspects of which were not accepted by Polanyi. Both are clear that the perception of raw sense-data in Russell's sense is not normal but is achieved only by an experimental approach which is seldom applied in everyday life, and that therefore in Russell's sense we would never have knowledge by acquaintance of anything but live in the world of ideas all the time. Polanyi wants to escape from this.

In his public lecture 'Recent Progress in the Theory of Vision', Helmholtz discussed and perhaps introduced into scientific discourse for the first time concepts which would play a role in the development of gestalt theory and the ideas of Polanyi, as well as in other competing trends of thought, namely unconscious inference, and the concept pairs *Wissen* and *Kennen* (the former being categorical knowledge, the latter being analogous to knowledge by acquaintance) and *Wissen* and *Können* (knowing that and knowing how).

Polanyi elsewhere argued that some visual illusions are not unbreakable but depend on experience. To take the most extreme example, the Ames room (which appears to make a small boy larger than a grown man because the viewer is given only a single perspective on a space which is not rectangular, but which is constructed to produce a perspectival illusion of a normal rectangular room) depends on our familiarity with rectangular rooms. Polanyi considers that a once-achieved integration of a particular set of clues can only be replaced by a superior one, which may or may not be available at any particular time. Seeing a strange configuration 'as' something familiar will always be preferred to

Helmholtz, 'Recent Progress'	*Polanyi*
The simple rule for all illusions of sight is this: *we always believe that we see such objects as would, under conditions of normal vision, produce the retinal image of which we are actually conscious.* If these images are such as could not be produced by any normal kind of observation, we judge of them according to their nearest resemblance; and in forming this judgement, we more easily neglect the parts of sensation which are imperfectly than those which are perfectly apprehended. When more than one interpretation is possible, we usually waver involuntarily between them; but it is possible to end this uncertainty by bringing the idea of any of the possible interpretations we choose as vividly as possible before the mind by a conscious effort of the will . . . These illusions obviously depend upon mental processes which may be described as false inductions. But there are, no doubt, judgements which do not depend upon our consciously thinking over former observations of the same kind, and examining whether they justify the conclusions which we form. I have, therefore, named these 'unconscious judgements'; and this term, though accepted by other supporters of the Empirical Theory, has excited much opposition, because, according to generally-accepted psychological doctrines, a *judgement*, or *logical conclusion*, is the culminating point of the conscious operations of the mind. But the judgements which play so great a part in the perceptions we derive from our	Once this basic distinction between explicit inference and tacit integration is clear, it throws new light on a 100-year old controversy. In 1867 Helmholtz offered to interpret perception as a process of unconscious inference, but this theory was generally rejected by psychologists, who pointed out that optical illusions are not destroyed by demonstrating their falsity. Psychologists had assumed, quite reasonably, that 'unconscious inference' had the same structure as a conscious explicit inference. But if we identify 'unconscious inference' with tacit integration, we have a kind of inference that is not damaged by adverse evidence, as explicit inference is. The difference between a deduction and an integration lies in the fact that deduction connects two focal items, the premises and consequents, while integration makes subsidiaries bear on a focus. Admittedly there is a purposive movement in a deduction – which is its essential tacit coefficient; but the deductive operation can be mechanically performed, while a tacit integration is intentional throughout, and, as such, can be carried out only by a conscious act of the mind. Brentano has taught that consciousness necessarily attends to an object and that only a conscious mental act can attend to an object. Our analysis of tacit knowing has amplified this view of consciousness. It tells us not only that consciousness is intentional but also that it always has roots from which it attends to its object. It includes a tacit awareness of its subsidiaries . . .

senses cannot be expressed in the ordinary form of logically analysed conclusions, and it is necessary to deviate somewhat from the beaten paths of psychological analysis in order to convince ourselves that we really have here the same kind of mental operation as that involved in conclusions usually recognised as such. There appears to me to be in reality only a superficial difference between the 'conclusions' of logicians and those inductive conclusions of which we recognise the result in conceptions we gain of the outer world through our sensations. The difference chiefly depends upon the former conclusions being capable of expression in words, while the latter are not; because, instead of words, they only deal with sensations and the memory of sensations. Indeed, it is just the impossibility of describing sensations, whether actual or remembered, in words, which makes it so difficult to discuss this department of psychology at all.

(Cited in Warren and Warren 1968, pp. 130 and 130–1)

David Hume maintained that, when in doubt, we must suspend judgment. This theory might apply to conclusions derived on paper, conclusions that can be manipulated at will – at least on paper. But our eyes continue to see a little boy taller than a grown man (although we know this must be false) as long as no feasible alternative integration is presented to our imagination. When we are presented with an alternative that appears to us to be more meaningful and so more true, a new perception will take place and correct our errors. Helmholtz could have answered his opponents on this score, but he would have had to admit that his 'unconscious inferences' were very different from conscious inferences.

(Polanyi and Prosch 1975, pp. 40–1 and 42)

Remember that Helmholtz tried to interpret perception as a process of inference, but that this was rejected, because optical illusions are not destroyed by demonstrating their falsity. Tacit inference is like this. The fusion of the two stereoscopic pictures to a single spatial image is not the outcome of an argument; and if its result is illusory, as it can well be, it will not be shaken by argument. The fusion of the clues to the image on which they bear is *not a deduction* but an *integration*.

(Polanyi 1969, p. 212)

seeing it as a confusing paradox, and so knowledge that an appearance is an illusion will often not lead to its disappearance. The illusions of incompatible angles and concave/convex spaces can only come alive for people who are trained in reading diagrams as pictures, and the immediacy of many nineteenth-century illusions of two competing faces or figures depends on familiarity with the engraving techniques of the time if both are to have equal saliency. The effect of the Ames room and the Ames chair both depend on familiarity with modern rooms and chairs, and only work from a specific viewing angle which forces a particular integration of the cues. Nevertheless, even from the forced viewing angle the Ames room effect would be lessened if the viewer had some way of manipulating the objects in the room, due to the tendency to map visual space onto tactile space.[10]

Helmholtz makes some statements which may have played a role in the development of Polanyi's thought on *physiognomy* in his special technical sense.

Helmholtz, 'Recent Progress'	*Polanyi*
Besides the knowledge which has to do with Notions, and is, therefore, capable of expression in words, there is another department of our mental operations, which may be described as knowledge of the relations of those impressions on the senses which are not capable of direct verbal expression. For instance when we say that we 'know' a man, a road, a fruit, a perfume, we mean that we have seen, or tasted, or smelt, these objects. We keep the sensible impression fast in our memory, and we shall recognise it again when it is repeated, but we cannot describe the impression in words, even to ourselves. And yet it is certain that this kind of knowledge [*Kennen*] may attain the highest degree of precision and certainty, and is so far not inferior to any knowledge [*Wissen*] which can be expressed in words; but it is not directly communicable, unless the object in question can be brought actually forward, or the impression it produces can be otherwise represented – as by drawing the portrait of a man instead of producing the man himself. (Cited in Warren and Warren 1968, p. 131)	A few years ago a distinguished psychiatrist demonstrated to his students a patient who was having a mild fit of some kind. Later the class discussed the question whether this had been an epileptic or a hystero-epileptic seizure. The matter was finally decided by the psychiatrist: 'Gentlemen,' he said, 'you have seen a true epileptic seizure. I cannot tell you how to recognize it: you will learn this by more extensive experience.' Clinical practitioners call the peculiar indescribable appearance of a pathological condition its *facies*; I shall call it a physiognomy, so as to relate it to the delicately varied expressions of the human face which we can likewise identify without being able to tell quite how we recognize them. We may describe as a physiognomy also the peculiar appearance of a species which can be recognized only 'aesthetically' and further include among physiognomies the characteristics of wines and blends of tea which only an expert can recognize. (Polanyi 1969, p. 121)

Working on the concept of *expertise* as developed by K. Anders Ericsson and his associates, Patel and Groen (1991) reported on an extensive series of investigations of the development of medical expertise. They concluded that the development of expertise is non-linear. They found that while accuracy of diagnosis increased throughout the process of training, there appeared to be a point at which the method by which diagnosis was achieved flipped over from backward to forward reasoning. This could possibly be mapped onto their finding that recall of relevant data rose continuously at first but later dropped off again. This appears to be evidence for a phase where the amount of knowledge available which can be applied to each case becomes too great to process, so that it becomes more efficient to switch from backward reasoning (systematic testing of a hypothesis) to forward reasoning (looking for disconfirming evidence of a hypothesis). However, at a higher level the ability to use 'backward reasoning' once again becomes important, where difficult cases appear which require simultaneous consideration of many anomalies or 'loose ends'. Thus, success at the level of acquiring enough information to be able to make the switch to forward reasoning successfully is not evidence of high skills in backward reasoning, so that some experts may be less able than others to deal with unusual cases.

We can map this finding onto the process of acquiring a repertoire of the *facies*, or physiognomies, of a variety of pathological conditions. The switch in reasoning method can be seen as a point at which the 'physiognomies' in Polanyi's sense, in this case those of medical syndromes, become gestalts which 'leap out' at the learners. Instead of explaining the discrepancy of the case from the healthy condition, the learners begin to see the pathological condition as basic and to look for evidence which is anomalous for the pathological condition. The authors do not believe that expert knowledge is simply a result of pattern recognition. It would be possible to explain this in terms of Polanyi's 'turning around', in which the switch is due not to a linear improvement in recognition of symptoms, but to a switch of reference point from normal-versus-pathological to standard-pathological-versus-anomalous.

Helmholtz discusses a form of knowing which is ingrained in the body and indissolubly linked with patterns of muscular activity. He describes this in terms which are analogous to the distinction of 'knowing that and knowing how' widely associated with Gilbert Ryle.[11] He places this within the *Kennen* type of knowledge, thus as a special kind of knowledge by acquaintance:

> It is an important part of the former kind of knowledge to be acquainted with the particular innervation of muscles, which is necessary in order to produce any effect we intend by moving our limbs. As children, we must learn to walk; we must afterwards learn how to skate or go on stilts, how to ride, or swim, or sing, or pronounce a foreign language. Moreover, observation of infants shows that they have to learn a number of things which afterwards they will know so well as entirely to forget that there

was ever a time when they were ignorant of them. For example, every one of us had to learn, when an infant, how to turn his eyes toward the light in order to see. This kind of 'knowledge' (*Kennen*) we also call 'being able' to do a thing (*können*), or 'understanding' how to do it (*verstehen*), as, 'I know how to ride', 'I am able to ride', or 'I understand how to ride'.

(Cited in Warren and Warren 1968, p. 131)

The conclusion of Helmholtz's lecture contains many disparate elements which can be found again in Polanyi's concerns:

The reader will see that these investigations have led us to a field of mental operations which has been seldom entered by scientific explorers. The reason is that it is difficult to express these operations in words. They have been hitherto most discussed in writings on aesthetics, where they play an important part as Intuition, Unconscious Ratiocination, Sensible Intelligibility, and such obscure designations. There lies under all these phrases the false assumption that the mental operations we are discussing take place in an undefined, obscure, half-conscious fashion; that they are, so to speak, mechanical operations, and thus subordinate to conscious thought, which can be expressed in language. I do not believe that any difference in kind between the two functions can be proved. The enormous superiority of knowledge which has become ripe for expression in language is sufficiently explained by the fact that, in the first place, speech makes it possible to collect together the experience of millions of individuals and thousands of generations, to preserve them safely, and by continual verification to make them gradually more and more certain and universal; while, in the second place, all deliberately combined actions of mankind, and so the greatest part of human power, depend on language. In neither of these respects can mere familiarity with phenomena (*das Kennen*) compete with the knowledge of them which can be communicated by speech (*das Wissen*); and yet it does not follow of necessity that the one kind of knowledge should be of a different nature from the other, or less clear in its operation.

(Cited in Warren and Warren 1968, p. 133)

In the decade following the publication of 'Recent Progress', Helmholtz was forced to concede that his use of the term 'unconscious judgement' had been unfortunate, but only because it had been used before by Schopenhauer in a different and unacceptable manner. Helmholtz continued to believe that he had discovered a real phenomenon:

Our sensations are only effects which are produced by external agents upon our organs, and the way in which such an effect is manifested, of course, depends essentially on the nature of the apparatus which is affected. As far as the quality of the external source of our perception gives us information about the characteristic nature of the external source of stimulation, it can be regarded as a symbol, but not as an image of this source. For an image some kind of identity with the portrayed object is demanded: for a statue, identity of form; for a drawing, identity of perspective projection in the field of vision; and for a picture, the additional identity of colors. A symbol however does not have to possess any kind of similarity with the object which it represents: the relation between them is confined to the fact that the same object, acting under the same circumstances, will produce the same symbol; and that unlike symbols thus always correspond to unlike influences.

(Cited in Warren and Warren 1968, p. 212)

This can be seen as a parallel to Polanyi's (1969, p. 214) statement:

I shall say that we observe external objects by being subsidiarily aware of the impact they make on our body and of the responses our body makes to them. All our conscious transactions with the world involve our subsidiary use of our body. And our body is the only aggregate of things of which we are aware almost exclusively in such a subsidiary manner.

Helmholtz continues by explaining that rather than being a picture of the world, our senses provide us with a network of tokens of those aspects of the world which affect us and which we can affect. This is so because we – living beings, in the evolutionary processes through time – have built up this network by attending and relying on those phenomena *within us* which bear a regular, lawlike relationship to what is happening outside, so that our attendance to them and reliance on them is evolutionarily useful (notwithstanding that the mechanisms involved may be imperfectly efficient and thus provide us with more or less data than we would wish):

Contrary to popular opinion, which accepts in good faith the complete truth of the images which our senses furnish us of external things, the morsel of similarity which we have acknowledged may appear quite insignificant. Actually it is not, for by it something of the greatest importance can be achieved, namely the representation of lawfulness in the processes of the real world. Every natural law states that preliminary conditions which are equivalent in a certain respect must have consequences which are equivalent in certain other respects. Since in our perceptual world equivalence is indicated by the identity of symbols, the law of nature that the same consequences follow from the same causes will have a corresponding law concerning consequences which are just as regular in the field of our perception.

(Cited in Warren and Warren 1968, pp. 212–13)

Helmholtz explained the problems which had arisen because of the use of the term *'unbewusster Schluss'* in a different sense from his own by Schopenhauer, the most influential philosopher of mid-nineteenth-century Germany. He makes clear that this term, which has been variously translated as unconscious *conclusion*, *judgement* or *inference*, is intended by him not as a special kind of thinking but as the most basic and universal kind of thinking. In this he is clearly working along parallel lines to Polanyi's emphasis on the tacit integration of clues as the underlying mechanism of all thought. It is clear that Helmholtz's discussion of visual illusions is an example of using pathological evidence to derive theories of normal operations, and that unconscious inference (as we have called it here) is not merely an explanation of the anomalies which bring it to our attention:

> In my earlier works I named the conceptual connections occurring in this process *unconscious conclusions*. Unconscious, in respect to the major premise based upon a sequence of experiences, each of which had long since disappeared from memory and entered consciousness only in the form of sensory impressions, not necessarily as sentences framed in words. New sensory impressions occurring in ongoing perception form the minor premise to which we apply the rule stamped in our mind by previous observations. Later I avoided that term 'unconscious conclusions', in order to escape from the entirely confused and unjustified concept – at any rate so it seems to me – which Schopenhauer and his disciples designate by this name. We are obviously concerned here with a basic process which underlies all that truly can be called thinking, although it lacks the critical sifting and completion of individual steps found in the scientific formulation of concepts and ideas.
>
> (Cited in Warren and Warren 1968, p. 220)

Breaking out in the progress of science

Polanyi's concepts of 'breaking out' and 'turning around' – that is to say, of extending our personal space to encompass the territory of theories built up by indwelling in the particulars of these theories and then of taking these theories as the raw material for further theories – may sound strange to the lay person, but they are not so ridiculous when we observe how theories of atomic structure, then of sub-atomic structure, and finally of the inner structure of sub-atomic particles have been constructed on the basis of one another, in each case initially without any immediate hope of obtaining verifiable evidence because of the lack of appropriate instruments, but with eventual vindication. Polanyi's own work on crystalline structures and on the distortion of materials proceeded in a similar fashion. Here we can see how Max Born, one of the leaders of the generation which developed quantum mechanics, expresses an idea in similar terms to Polanyi, probably neither as a result of influence nor by coincidence, but because both worked within a tradition which derived these ideas from Helmholtz.

Max Born	***Polanyi***
It presupposes that our sense impressions are not a permanent hallucination, but the indications of, or signals from, an external world which exists independently of us. Although these signals change and move in a most bewildering way, we are aware of objects with invariant properties. The set of these invariants of our sense impressions is the physical reality which our mind constructs in a perfectly unconscious way. This chair here looks different with each movement of my head, each twinkle of my eye, yet I perceive it as the same chair. Science is nothing else than the endeavour to construct these invariants where they are not obvious. If you are not a trained scientist and look through a microscope you see nothing other than specks of light and colour, not objects; you have to apply the technique of biological science, consisting in altering conditions, observing correlations, etc., to learn that what you see is a tissue with cancer cells, or something like that. The words denoting things are applied to permanent features of observation or observational invariants. (Born 1964, pp. 103–4)	If explicit rules can operate only by virtue of a tacit coefficient, the ideal of exactitude has to be abandoned. What power of knowing can take its place? The power which we exercise in the act of perception. The capacity of scientists to perceive the presence of lasting shapes as tokens of reality in nature differs from the capacity of our ordinary perception only by the fact that it can integrate shapes presented to it in terms which the perception of ordinary people cannot readily handle. Scientific knowing consists in discerning Gestalten that are aspects of reality. I have here called this 'intuition'; in later writings I have described it as the tacit coefficient of a scientific theory, by which it bears on experience, as a token of reality. Thus it foresees yet indeterminate manifestations of the experience on which it bears. (Polanyi 1964a, p. 10)

At the time of writing, the latest example of the process described is found in the discovery of new methods for estimating the amount of 'dark matter' in the universe. As far as we are aware, this matter has no directly observable effect 'on' us, but its existence has to be posited to explain the rates of acceleration of galaxies, rates of movement of which we had no concept a hundred years ago, and rates of the movement of objects of which we had no concept two hundred years ago, when the 'Milky Way', the 'Galaxy', our own local galaxy, was the only exemplar of what we now recognise as its 'class' of objects, of which we were even vaguely aware.

Gestalt

Polanyi several times stated that his philosophy was a continuation of the approach of the school of gestalt theorists. This might seem to relate only to the gestalt theory of perception, but comparison of Koffka's overview of the significance of the gestalt approach will show that much of Polanyi's social and personalist philosophy was a direct continuation of the wider concerns of the gestaltists. At the same time it will be apparent that what the gestaltists saw as a distinction between instinct and thinking reappears in Polanyi as a distinction between animal thought and thought mediated by language.

The gestalt theory arose from the recognition that associationist conceptions about how the stream of perception is organised to produce our generally clear distinctions of figure and ground, of significant and insignificant, are some-how inadequate. The movement was inspired by Christian von Ehrenfels, who demonstrated in 1890 that complex perceptual units such as a melody, or, of particular importance for Polanyi, a physiognomy such as a person's face, are perceived as a 'gestalt', a technical term often translated as 'configuration'. This means that it is the total combination of elements which is decisive in deciding whether a particular configuration is the 'same' as a remembered one, or whether a novel configuration belongs in a particular class of entities. Because they decided that associationism could not explain how wholes were rapidly built up out of the data of sight or how a succession of notes was experienced as a melody, they turned to the contemporary theory of electrical fields for an explanation.

The empirical aspect of gestaltist research on vision, inspired by Ehrenfels, has stood the test of time, and any modern work will list and demonstrate their laws of organisation, such as continuity, closure, proximity and similarity.[12] However, their experimental situations were based on a fixed gaze and a fixed frontal display, and did not investigate perception of a moving subject in a mobile environment.[13] Later research has vindicated the gestaltist criticism of older global associationism but has looked for intermediate steps in the analysis of perceptual data, a kind of 'chunking' which constructs boundaries and contours in a piecemeal way and then pieces them together. This may be comparable to Polanyi's 'integration of clues', and also to Helmholtz's 'unconscious inference', and is certainly a better starting point for explaining inescapable optical illusions which arise from problems in interpretation of unusual boundaries and joins. In regard to music their empirical evidence has not survived as well. Petermann (1932, pp. 226–31) reports evidence that the apparent identity of melodies through various transpositions is only valid for a limited range of key changes, and that beyond this the balance between the individual sounds begins to alter so that the abstract structure is no longer perceived as the same. The perceived similarities which Ehrenfels and the gestaltists had originally discovered in music can be explained as an artefact of the systems of scales, which are different from culture to culture, and which lead individuals to have certain expectations about music equivalent to those which we have for language.

Petermann (1932, pp. 304–5) argues that in making the gestalt a primary datum, which they claim makes the sensationalist or associationist theory of knowledge superfluous, the gestalt theorists have in fact reverted to the *eidola* theory of Democritus, who thought that objects generate images of themselves which act upon the sense organs to reproduce these images in the mind. The gestalt theory may be seen as inspiring, but not as genuinely leading to, the contemporary understanding that perception involves mechanisms which use specifically targeted methods to isolate figures from their ground and to categorise them.

The gestaltists' field theory of how perception works is by contrast completely discredited and is rarely referred to, which to some extent allows them to appear in a better light than would be the case if it were more widely known. Petermann's *The Gestalt Theory and the Problem of Configuration* was a devastating critique from within the same tradition, and although the gestaltists continued to publish, they had no direct followers. Polanyi's own work, while several times termed a continuation of their inspiration, is really a continuation of attempting to explain their empirical results rather than an adoption of their specific explanatory devices. Even so, the association with gestalt theory became a negative factor in the reception of Polanyi's work in the 1950s. Piaget several times discusses the gestaltists as precursors of his own interpretation of structuralism, but obviously regards them as a spent force.[14]

The gestalt theory is based on the assumption that pre-reflective human life is a series of responses to the active influence of the environment. The mechanism proposed for this influence is the field theory, which is now forgotten. It is posited that humanity historically liberated itself from the power of the fields by the linked development of thinking and language. In the gestalt theory the power of thought arises from the way in which it liberates humanity from the power of the fields, since we can think about things in their absence, and so in isolation from their overwhelming power over us. Although Polanyi accepted the failure of the gestalt school explanation of the power and origin of images, he follows them in seeing conscious thought and scientific discovery as arising out of and remaining rooted in the more basic ways of knowing.[15]

Koffka	*Polanyi*
Exaggerating and schematising the differences, we can say: in the pre-scientific stage man behaves in a situation as the situation tells him to behave. To primitive man each thing says what it is and what he ought to do with it: a fruit says 'Eat me'; water says 'Drink me'; thunder says 'Fear me'; and woman says 'Love me' . . . This world is limited, but, up to a point, manageable, knowledge is direct and quite unscientific, in many cases perfectly true, but in many others hopelessly wrong. And man slowly discovered the errors in his original world. He learned to distrust what things told him, and gradually he forgot the language of birds and stones. Instead he developed a new activity which he called thinking. And this new activity brought him great advantages. He could think out the consequences of events and actions and thereby make himself free of past and present. By thinking he created knowledge in the sense of scientific knowledge, knowledge which was no longer a knowledge of individual things, but of universals. (Koffka 1935, p. 7)	Thus to speak a language is to commit ourselves to the double indeterminacy due to our reliance both on its formalism and on our own continued reconsideration of this formalism bearing on our experience. For just as, owing to the ultimately tacit character of all our knowledge, we remain forever unable to say all that we know, so also, in view of the tacit character of meaning, we can never quite know what is implied in what we say. Before proceeding further, I must return for a moment to the point where I set out my programme for Parts Two and Three. I proposed there to bring the conception of truth in accordance with the following three facts which became broadly apparent from the start: (1) Nearly all knowledge by which man surpasses the animals is acquired by language. (2) The operations of language rely ultimately on our tacit intellectual powers which are continuous with those of the animals. (3) These inarticulate acts of intelligence strive to satisfy self-set standards and reach their conclusions by accrediting their own success. (Polanyi 1958, pp. 95–6)

This leads us to the topic of the continued relevance of the passion of discovery in scientific investigation, and the dynamic which this lends to a process which is only presented in theory as disinterested and self-sufficient.

The dynamic of the tacit component of scientific theory

Polanyi begins *Personal Knowledge* with a discussion of the openness of scientific discoveries to future elaboration. This section has been interpreted as envisaging a mystical vision of future knowledge because critics have not grasped Polanyi's wider theory. They have taken the standard criteria of scientific propositional discourse to apply, although Polanyi argues that they are not really what happens. He also argues that such criteria should not be dogmatically accepted as prescriptive, but the critics have failed to see that he is primarily denying that they do actually describe how real science is done and has been done in the past. Therefore, critics suppose that the theories of Copernicus, Galileo and Newton are genuinely axiomatic and that Polanyi is smuggling something into them when he says that they are not merely the building blocks of more developed theories but contain intimations of later theories. But Polanyi is really saying that the apparently axiomatic basis of these theories contains a large tacit component, and that the dynamic of these components propels theories towards future developments, which may or may not be valid or accurate, but when they are found or considered to be so, it is in large part due to this original tacit component. A later summary of the content of the first chapter of *Personal Knowledge*, taken from the introduction to the second edition of *Science, Faith and Society* (1964a), is here set in parallel with a passage from Alfred Schutz *et al.* Although Schutz *et al.* are not discussing scientific theories, their description of how 'preknowledge of as yet unapperceived properties' of objects, 'preorganized by previous experiencing acts', can play a dynamic formative role in 'additional experiencing acts' which reveal 'ever new additional determinations of the same objectivity' is offered here as evidence not of influence but of a wider common background of thought on which both Schutz *et al.* and Polanyi are drawing.

Schutz, Type and Eidos	*Polanyi*
According to Husserl, the world and the individual objects in it are always experienced by us as having been preorganized by previous experiencing acts of the most various kinds. In any experience, even that of an objectivity apperceived for the first time, a preknowledge of as yet unapperceived properties of the object is involved, a preknowledge which might be undetermined or incompletely determined as to its content, but which will never be entirely empty. In other words, any experience carries along an experiential horizon which refers to the possibility (in subjective terms,	I first analysed the process of knowing, as is usual, in isolation. There are an infinite number of mathematical formulae which will cover any series of numerical observations. Any additional future observations can still be accounted for by an infinite number of formulae. Moreover, no mathematical function connecting instrument readings can ever constitute a scientific theory. Future instrument readings cannot ever be predicted. But this is merely symptom of a deeper inadequacy, namely, that the explicit content of a theory fails to account for the guidance it affords to future

to the faculty) not merely to explicate step by step objectivity as it is given in actual apperception, but also to obtain by additional experiencing acts ever new additional determinations of the same objectivity. This infinite open horizon of the actual experience functions as the scope of anticipated possibilities of further determination; yet in spite of their undetermined generality these anticipations are, according to Husserl, nevertheless *typically* determined by their *typical* prefamiliarity, as *typically* belonging, that is, to the total horizon of the same and identifiable objectivity, the actually apperceived properties of which show the same general *type*. (Schutz, Type and Eidos in Schutz 1966, p. 94)	discoveries. To hold a natural law to be true is to believe that its presence will manifest itself in an indeterminate range of yet unknown and perhaps yet unthinkable consequences. It is to regard the law as a real feature of nature which, as such, exists beyond our control. We meet here with a new definition of reality. Real is that which is expected to reveal itself indeterminately in the future. Hence an explicit statement can bear on reality only by virtue of the tacit coefficient associated with it. This conception underlies all my writings. (Polanyi 1964a, pp. 9–10)

Dilthey and phenomenology

Polanyi acknowledged that phenomenology was part of the movement of thought initiated by Wilhelm Dilthey, within which he also situated both the gestalt theory and his own work. Polanyi thought that Dilthey and the other thinkers of his age were wrong to believe that there was a fundamental methodological divide between the natural sciences and the social and historical sciences:

> [S]ince all understanding is tacit knowing, all understanding is achieved by indwelling. The idea developed by Dilthey and Lipps, that we can know human beings and works of art only by indwelling, can thus be justified. But we see now also that these authors were mistaken in distinguishing indwelling from observation as practised in the natural sciences. The difference is only a matter of degree: indwelling is less deep when observing a star than when understanding men or works of art. The theory of tacit knowing establishes a continuous transition from the natural sciences to the humanities. It bridges the gap between the 'I-It' and the 'I-Thou', by rooting both in the subject's 'I-Me' awareness of his own body, which represents the highest degree of indwelling.
>
> (Polanyi 1969, p. 160)

For Polanyi, all knowing is rooted in tacit knowing and therefore in the active body, since all knowledge arises from our interpretation of things taking place inside the body as tokens of what is taking place outside. This is true equally of both social and natural events, and therefore it is true equally of both the social and the natural sciences, which are a higher stage of reflection on those events and their lawful structure. For Polanyi, Dilthey was the pioneer in describing the process of indwelling, but he confined himself to the sympathetic indwelling of one person in the particulars of the lives of others, particularly as a method of historical and psychological science. Polanyi argues that this was a false dichotomy, and that the process of indwelling is our only way of knowing the world outside ourselves. He stated this in connection with his acknowledgement of the role of Dilthey for him, which simultaneously illustrated his recognition that in the English-speaking world the importance of Dilthey had never been grasped and had since been overshadowed by the reputation of some of his followers, such as Husserl and Heidegger.

> Dilthey has since been richly interpreted for English readers by Hodges. His work forms part of a great intellectual network which includes phenomenology and existentialism and has transformed the whole climate of philosophy on the Continent of Europe. Out of it has issued modern Gestalt psychology, which I myself am trying to restore to its function as a theory of knowledge adumbrated in its philosophical origins. Many of my statements are reminiscent of this movement; but let me recall that its thought was based throughout on the exclusion of the natural sciences from its scope.
>
> (Polanyi 1959, p. 102)

A passage may be reproduced from Dilthey's major presentation of his scientific programme, the preface to the *Introduction to the Sciences of Mind*, which will give a very clear idea of what Polanyi felt he had in common with Dilthey and what he hoped to achieve in *Personal Knowledge*: to situate the process of scientific discovery within the 'totality of our being'. (In Dilthey's text the word 'science' refers to the sciences of the mind and of man, in line with the restriction of Dilthey's approach to these areas, as Polanyi complained of in the previous extract.)

> The method of the following exposition is therefore as follows: I bring every element in our present-day abstract scientific thinking into relation with the whole nature of man as revealed by experience, by linguistic and historical study, and I look for the connections between the one and the other. The result is to show that the most important elements in the way we picture and know reality, such as personal identity, the external world, individuals outside ourselves, their life in time and their interactions – all these can be explained in terms of this whole nature of man, in which

volition, feeling, and cognition are only different sides of a single real life-process. It is not by the assumption of rigid a priori principles belonging to our cognitive faculty, but only by starting with the totality of our being and tracing the course of its development, that we can answer the questions which we all have to address to philosophy.

(Dilthey cited in Hodges 1944, pp. 113–14)

The dynamic of indwelling and scientific discovery

Our grasp of the qualities of distant things is the result of actions going on within ourselves which we do not directly experience but of which we have awareness as indicators of those distant things. We can extend the range of these relationships with tools and probes, and with instruments and heuristics. Our body is our way of knowing about what is outside our body as much or more than we know about what is inside it. By dwelling in our body we also dwell in the entire nexus of which our body is the centre. Polanyi now draws on research which shows that we can begin to control tiny bodily actions of which we are normally completely unaware if we are put into a situation where these have an effect on the outside world. Hefferline and his collaborators[16] created a feedback loop so that an unpleasant noise would cease when human subjects flexed a minor muscle. After some trials the sound was regularly silenced, although the subjects were unaware of being able to influence this occurrence. This was the beginning of the research which later led to the conscious use of biofeedback to allow humans to exercise small muscles in patterns which would never normally be activated consciously. Polanyi considers that this phenomenon is another instance of our ability to extend the boundaries of our body by establishing correlations between things inside our body which we can become aware of and some regular patterns of change in the outer world. He considers that this also explains why it is that all our senses require some degree of learning to become usefully operative, since they are systems of active adjustment to the structure of the external stimuli. He summarises:

> Our body is the ultimate instrument of all our external knowledge, whether intellectual or practical. In all our waking moments we are *relying* on our awareness of contacts of our body with things outside for *attending* to these things. Our own body is the only thing in the world which we normally never experience as an object, but experience always in terms of the world to which we are attending from our body. It is by making this intelligent use of our body that we feel it to be our body, and not a thing outside.
>
> (Polanyi 1966, pp. 15–16)

To address this last point first: the experience of feeling that one of our limbs is not *our* limb arises from the cessation of information from that limb about the external world. We feel that our body parts are part of us because we experience the world through them, and when this experience ceases, the limb becomes something alien and strange. If our limb is immobilised for some time, then although the nerves are intact, the brain interprets the constant lack of fresh data as a signal that the limb is absent, and can delete the reception sites for this data.[17] Polanyi's more general point is that indwelling or participation is the general form of our knowledge of the world, and that it is through the processing and active transformation of the information within the body through the from–to processes of focal and subsidiary awareness that we build up this relationship of indwelling in the 'external' world. Polanyi then stresses (1966, p. 17) that our indwelling in ideas such as moral teachings or scientific theories is of the same nature. He reaches another transition in his thinking:

> The identification of tacit knowing with indwelling involves a shift of emphasis in our conception of tacit knowing. We had envisaged tacit knowing in the first place as a way to know more than we can tell. We identified the two terms of tacit knowing, the proximal and the distal, and recognized the way we attend *from* the first *to* the second, thus achieving an integration of particulars to a coherent entity to which we are attending . . . [this integration of particulars as an interiorization] now becomes a means of making certain things function as the proximal terms of tacit knowing, so that instead of observing them in themselves, we may be aware of them in their bearing on the comprehensive unity they constitute.
>
> (Polanyi 1966, pp. 17–18)

We first need to remind ourselves that Polanyi's interest in our ability to 'know more than we can tell' arises initially from dissatisfaction with the 'critical' (Cartesian) project of building up our entire knowledge of the world from a few clear and distinct ideas in imitation of the method of geometry. The theory of tacit knowing explains in contrast that we always begin any scientific investigation on the basis of a mass of unstated assumptions about the world. We can subsequently turn around and unpick some of these unstated assumptions but we can never be sure that we have identified and examined all of them. But in the meantime our heuristics and theories create a new extension of the boundaries of our world, and in this extended world those of our heuristics which we indwell begin to become proximal starting points for the discovery of additional distal focuses of our attention. This is the process of scientific discovery, but also of all moral, artistic, philosophical and religious discoveries. This is the process of 'breaking out' (extending the limits of our world) and of 'turning around' (taking our discoveries as the starting point of new discoveries) which have become accepted by some of Polanyi's followers but which have received little critical notice by non-'Polanyians', with the exception of an essay by Robert Cohen (1971).

Cohen sees the problem with Polanyi as being to discover what it is that he is trying to do. For Cohen, Polanyi's theories cannot be seen as a theory of knowledge, which must always end in justifying the end product of a given body of knowledge: rather, Polanyi is to be seen as developing a theory of discovery and learning. In this context Cohen sees Polanyi as a participant in the broader movement of logical positivism. Although this might have horrified Polanyi, there is some evidence that not all members of the Vienna Circle were as distant from Polanyi as Carnap or Popper:

> The only reasonable conception seems to be that, to varying degrees, instinct, intuition, and weighing and analyzing reason concur in all discoveries, not only physical and biological, but also in such areas as philology and history. The whole concept of an opposition between instinct and intellect seems so artificial to us that we think it is due neither to a lucky instinct, nor to a sharp intellect.
>
> (Mises 1968, p. 61)

Cohen takes up Polanyi on a phrase which brings us back to the roots of Polanyi's thinking on Helmholtz as we have attempted to develop them above. Cohen asks:

> Polanyi uses a very revealing and profound phrase 'tacit powers' to notice that we convert the impact between our bodies and the things that come our way into a comprehension of their meaning, so that our active role as knowers is a part of the subject–object relationship in given contexts. The very expression 'we convert the impact of things into a comprehension of their meaning' hides a little obscurity of great import. Is it our comprehension of their meaning? The meaning of what? Do we make or *read* the meaning in or of the things that come our way? Their meaning for us or their meaning in themselves? If it's their meaning *for us*, have we made it into *their* meaning for us? And thereby partly made them? If it's their meaning in themselves, what provides our cucs?
>
> (Cohen 1971, p. 142)

We can begin to resolve this question by recalling that there is no empty theatre of consciousness into which these 'impacts' intrude. The 'tacit powers' we possess have arisen in evolutionary time by the correlation of actions with phenomena within the body of our ancestors. These phenomena are – in most cases – caused by external events. By establishing patterns of action which 'respond' – this word is already running ahead to the outcome of the process – on the occasion of these 'impacts', we make these internal phenomena into tokens of external processes. This 'stimulus–response' action becomes more complex in millennia of evolution. There is thereby a constant mutual selection between those phenomena which affect us in the sense of being perceptible and to which we can in some way react and the lawful relationship which these phenomena have to some process which affects our ability to survive and for which these tokens then come to serve as signals. To use the word 'meaning' here is to insert an ambiguity because of the discrepancy between what meaning is when we are reacting to phenomena in the world and what it means within systems of formal thought. But for Polanyi, systems of formal thought are still part of the passionate engagement of humans with the universe, and it is this totality which Polanyi wishes to grasp in line with the programme of Dilthey as cited above.

In the next chapter we will attempt to sketch a provisional taxonomy of the components of the tacit component of all knowledge and skill.[18] This might seem to lead to a checklist approach to the background elements which are necessary to carry out specific tasks in a work environment, and so to make concretisation of the approach developed here equivalent to instrumentalisation. The absorption of the full import of Polanyi's work is a long and difficult process, but leads to the realisation that human skills arise from an open-ended process of discovery and self-discovery within indwelling and commitment to contexts and situations. This suggests that taking Polanyi seriously would mean that alongside issues of economic compensation and human respect, workplace contestation necessarily involves the passionate involvements of human beings in their work and its wider meaning.

4 Implicit, tacit and explicit components of personal knowledge

In this chapter we will attempt to sketch the possible elements of an inventory of the tacit components of all use of skills and practical knowledge. We will draw on the results of the previous chapter but rearrange the material in a pattern amenable to being used as a template for the practical analysis of the skills used in different everyday activities. We will continue to draw a distinction between use and learning for each kind of skill, in so far as conscious attention plays a different role in the acquisition and the application of skills. An equivalent distinction between implicit and explicit learning of knowledge will be sketched, although it should be remembered, first, that the content of explicit and implicit learning may not match exactly, so there is a possibility of divergence; second, that in different circumstances there may or may not be a pathway by which explicit learning subsequently becomes implicit, so in some cases explicit learning must always be supplemented by a separate phase of implicit learning even if the content does match; and, third, that all actual conditions of the use of skills and knowledge may be sub-optimal, so that circumstances discovered must not be taken as unchangeable.

Implicit learning and implicit knowledge

Implicit learning as originally proposed by Arthur Reber in 1967 has undergone a substantial evolution since 1995.[1] There seems little room for doubt that there is such a thing as implicit learning, understood as learning which takes place with some attention being paid to the phenomena about which learning takes place, but without conscious attention being paid to those aspects of the phenomena which are learned about. Since consciousness and language are evolutionarily later phenomena, it follows that implicit learning must be the oldest form of learning and the most basic. This would suggest that it could also be the most reliable. However, in humans it would seem that the survival value of consciousness has been so great that the conscious mechanisms have acquired first claim on the resources of the systems of perception. In laboratory experiments, rates of implicit learning fall drastically when distraction is used to ensure that conscious attention is required to be directed elsewhere. Implicit learning thus can take place only when there is spare capacity in the mechanisms of perception and where some attention is paid to the phenomena about which learning will take place. This is not in itself a controversial finding, since all learning must use real resources which are not infinite, otherwise we would have total recall of everything we have ever perceived. It explains the way in which acclimatisation to a new environment must necessarily proceed gradually, since familiarisation with one level of new phenomena frees up attentional resources to begin to absorb further less salient aspects of the novel surroundings. Accepting this process would be equivalent to Polanyi's *commitment* and *indwelling*, while an obsessive concern with escaping the environment will block absorption of the minutiae of it.

The controversial aspect of implicit learning appears to centre on the nature of the 'implicit knowledge' which is learned. Reber originally proposed that the knowledge embodied in the learners after learning was in the form of an abstract representation of an abstract body of relationships between different aspects of the phenomena learned about (which nevertheless remained inaccessible to the direct introspection of the learner and was only expressed by forced choices). During the past decade the view has become more prevalent that the knowledge acquired is in the form of discrete 'chunks' expressing the relationships between individual pairs (or triads) of elements in the arrays of phenomena learned about.

This must remain a distinction without a difference so long as we do not know how explicit knowledge is encoded in the brain. Thus we may think that we have a map of the London Underground in our brain, built up by years of studying the maps displayed in Underground stations and published in atlases and diaries, while in someone else's brain, or in another part of our brain, there may be a body of implicit learning acquired by actually using the Underground without paying attention to the structure of the system. We may think that implicit knowledge about the Underground is stored in the form of 'chunks', whereas our map is instantly accessible as an image in our brain which results from mentally 'looking' at our stored map, but how do we know that this map is not stored in the form of exactly the same kind of chunks which our brain then rapidly assembles into a map? Indeed, how do we know that the image in our head which we introspectively inspect is not just like our visual image, an exact part at the centre of our attention and a confabulated pseudo-map outside this area, which is upgraded whenever we shift our introspective centre of attention elsewhere within the map?[2]

Nevertheless, it seems established that there are indeed two stores or locations of knowledge, one explicit in the sense that we can consciously call it up, sometimes only with a struggle if we have not used it for a long time, and another which is learned implicitly and to which our conscious brain has no access, so that we only draw on the 'knowledge' located there when we act instinctively or, as in the experiments, when we are forced to 'guess' or to choose between alternatives with no other aid. To deny that the resource on which we draw in these cases is 'knowledge' either because it is not consciously accessible or because it does not have the structure of a system of deductions based on given axioms is to prejudge questions about the status and use of both implicit and explicit knowledge.

The important aspect of the most recent research is that which appears to confirm one thing about implicit learning, namely that it is contextually labelled. In other words, even if the body of knowledge stored about a particular context does not have the structure of a coherent logical diagram, the 'chunks' of knowledge about particular contexts are somehow kept apart from those relevant to other contexts. This is essential to the mechanism by which signals and clues are taken to mean different things in different contexts and at different stages of operations and processes.

Reber has acknowledged the contribution of Michael Polanyi (1958) and Friedrich von Hayek (1962) to the early formulation of the problems of implicit learning.[3] Polanyi's concept of tacit knowledge can be seen to cover knowledge acquired in two different ways: that which is first acquired explicitly and later through routine becomes internalised and tacit ('skills'); and that which is acquired by 'osmosis', actually by implicit inference from data and stimuli which may not be consciously registered or regarded as meaningful. The latter process is 'implicit learning' in Reber's sense.[4]

Reber (1993, p. 88) hypothesises that implicit systems would have the following characteristics:

1 **Robustness** . . . robust in the face of disorders and dysfunctions that compromise explicit learning and explicit memory.
2 **Age independence** . . . compared with explicit learning, implicit acquisition processes should show few effects of age and developmental level.
3 **Low variability** . . . population variances should be much smaller when implicit processes are measured than when explicit processes are.
4 **IQ independence** . . . implicit tasks should show little concordance with measures of 'intelligence' assessed by standard psychometric instruments . . .
5 **Commonality of process** . . . underlying processes of implicit learning should show cross-species commonality.

Essentially, since explicit, formal methods of learning and communication are all evolutionarily later than implicit methods, it follows that they will be less robust and therefore show greater variability between individuals and contexts. Implicit systems will operate in a greater variety of situations, their variation with age will not map onto that age-variation which is specific to the phases of the learning of formal symbolisation, their variability will not map onto the variability in facility of using these symbolic processes. The obvious implication is that learning-by-doing will be applicable in a wider set of contexts than formal learning.

Implicit learning thus understood would not be a second-class form of learning. On the contrary, it would seem to be preferable for many basic skills to be learned in this way, since learning would be less age and IQ sensitive and more robust in the face of distraction. Learning-by-doing without accompanying explicit instruction may come close to implicit learning in achieving these goals. Precisely because implicit learning is robust, however, there is a problem if the wrong things can be learned. In the past, learning within tradition converged on a consensus since the artefactual context of tools and materials strongly guided the learning towards the accepted outcomes, as did the learner's familiarity with the items to be made. The challenge would be to find equivalent structures which guide implicit learning in a rapidly changing world.

The implicit context of learning

In his critique of the 'implicit learning' school derived from Reber, Shanks (2005) made allowance for the existence of other forms of implicit learning which did not carry the burden of producing implicit abstract knowledge, some of which are discussed in the overview by Knowlton (2005) in the same handbook. Knowlton (2005, pp. 67–71) lists five varieties of implicit learning, all of which contribute to building up a picture of how commitment and indwelling in Polanyi's sense can work, with the advantage that it is possible to see how different individuals could converge on the same effective patterns of response to particular environments through different pathways. These are:

1 **Priming** Part of the effect of implicit learning in Reber's work was ascribed by his critics to the effect of priming. If we nevertheless take up the apparent confirmation of the ability of Reber's subjects to 'code-switch' between different patterns of learning, we can see priming as something which is itself context dependent. This means that fluency of interpreting data can be differentially triggered or inhibited by contextually varied patterns of priming. This is precisely what we need if objectively similar phenomena are to be fluently interpreted as having different significance within different contexts, processes or phases of processes. This also helps to explain how rapid environmental change can confuse us and lead to misinterpretation and false triggers through the subconscious effects of unusual patterns of priming. The challenge would be to maintain equivalent structures of priming data in order to facilitate rapid cross-contextual transfer of implicit learning in a rapidly changing world.

2 **Sequence learning** One of Reber's team's experiments involved serial reaction time tasks. Subjects were found to be able to 'learn' sequences of which they were not consciously aware, as revealed by the relative difficulty which they experienced in learning new tasks with similar or dissimilar sequence structures. The experiment is described by Knowlton (2005, p. 367) in these terms: 'Rather than a series of motor movements, it appears

that subjects are learning a series of locations.' This seems to mean that subjects are not learning a sequence of response motor movements, so that they will not perform badly if asked to respond using a different configuration of keys or switches, but it appears to overlook the fact that eye movements are themselves motor movements, so that a pattern of expectations expressed in glancing in a particular direction may well be learned as a pattern of muscular activity. It is not clear whether we can have purely internal representations of 'locations' without some associated representation of movement. However, as with Reber's own work, we do not need to decide finally whether the 'implicit knowledge' is abstract (as Knowlton considers possible, p. 368 column 2) or whether it is in the form of chunks.

3 **Preference learning** From the point of view of providing an underpinning for Polanyi's theories, this subject appears to provide two separate approaches. One aspect of preference learning is the 'mere exposure' effect, which means that subjects will more often than not prefer a known stimulus to an unknown one, even if they have no conscious memory of it. This is sometimes explained as a 'safety' effect, as any known phenomenon which is not directly associated with a danger is seen as safer than an unknown one. In any case, the effect can be used in forced choice texts to expose the subject's implicit memory since they will often prefer a known item over an unknown one even when they have no conscious recall of it. This would be an element of Polanyi's 'commitment' whereby we make contexts into our contexts.

However, Knowlton also reports experiments in which preferences were found to change over time. In one experiment subjects were initially asked to rank ten prints in order of preference. In a subsequent phase they were asked on two occasions to rank selected pairs of prints from the previous group. The prints which were preferred in this second phase of the test tended to be ranked even more highly than in the first test when the first test was repeated, and those which had been 'rejected' were subsequently ranked even lower than initially. Bearing in mind that the rankings were initially subjective, this suggests that if objective criteria were used, there would still be a tendency to view twice-confirmed objects more highly and twice-rejected ones less highly. This could be a source of the diagnostic errors caused by giving excessive weight to recent cases, but in some circumstances it could also have a positive effect if the underlying phenomena were themselves dynamic so that the recent-case bias is valuable.

4 **Habit learning** Habit is used here not in the sense of routine, but in that of the creation of fixed associations. This section is of great interest to us precisely because it tackles a subject in regard to which one would normally expect human beings to exhibit an explicit rather than an implicit approach. Since human beings are presumed mostly to form conscious associations,

which would undermine the testing of the forming of unconscious associations, a special test method was devised. Knowlton reports an experiment in which subjects were presented with combinations of cues, whereby each combination was related to particular outcomes only in a probabilistic way. Although the subjects were confused by receiving 20–40 per cent negative replies to their guesses, they gravitated towards the most likely outcome for each combination. Amnesiac subjects showed the same degree of learning over a series of trials, apparently indicating that conscious memory could not be the method used. The importance of this is that things which are indeed learned consciously may also be learned unconsciously simultaneously, and the memories concerned may be accessed and updated by the unconscious channel, meaning that our evaluation of objects and processes may be influenced by both conscious and unconscious conclusions, giving rise to the 'hunch' which is sometimes superior to the calculated logical response.

5   **Category learning** Knowlton takes the example that a chicken and a sparrow are both birds, but that a sparrow is more easily recognised as a bird because it is closer to the 'prototype' of a bird. This suggests that we do not classify by filtering through the categories of a definition, but by similarity to a prototype. Once again the learning of prototypes by amnesiacs who have no conscious memory of new learning is taken as evidence that we establish prototypes of new categories by implicit learning.[5] For our purposes the relevance of this would be that it is necessary to suppose that explicit instruction based on formal definitions is likely to be ineffective in eradicating the influence of alternative implicit learning which is in fact based on prototyping.

This review of different types of implicit learning suggests that in any attempt to distinguish, categorise and analyse the different components of the tacit component of any body of skills and knowledge or any competency, we might need to consider some or all of the following points:

- What are the priming characteristics of the work environment which might make a difference to the way in which the implicitly learned elements of the skill are primed and made more accessible to recall or activation at different stages of the process?
- What are the manifest or internalised expressions of sequence learning which might have an effect on the effectiveness of learning and executing the skill?
- What degree of explicit tuition or structured reflection on the variants of the materials and constellations of features present in the work is necessary to overcome 'mere exposure' and 'most recent cases' effects and help practitioners converge on an agreed ranking of the options or indicators present in the work?

- Is explicit instruction superior or inferior in producing the correct habits of associating particular combinations of cues with particular eventualities or outcomes within the work? Does mixing the two approaches help to converge on the correct practices or does it confuse the practitioners?
- Is prototype-formation a help or a hindrance in learning the skill; and if the latter, can it be combated by explicit instruction in a wider typology of the objects or processes of the work?

This is not meant to suggest that these kinds of questions are in substance completely new and that they are not in many cases already implicitly dealt with in the training for any particular competency. A template for analysing the tacit component of skills and competencies must develop a systematic approach. We must also remember that many competencies are not necessarily optimally developed at present.

Action faster than thought

Another area of learning with at least an implicit dimension is action learning, in which the actions in question must be carried out at speeds faster than conscious thought could monitor or control them.[6] Learning and using such action schemes and combinations of them may involve conscious thought, first in selecting repertoires of sub-units of movements, and then in choosing the best time to begin. Improvement in performance may also be subject to conscious reflection and interaction with mentors. Nevertheless, there must be some degree of implicit learning involved. This may be of two distinct types; in other words, these phenomena may reveal to us the existence of two distinct mechanisms. One, already discussed above in connection with hammering a nail, is the mechanism of responding to feedback from an ongoing process. In a wide range of manipulative, steering or controlling activities, and in sport and dance, it seems that the conscious mind must take the role of observing whether the action is proceeding adequately, while the fine adjustments of the body to the environment are carried out by the body or by areas of the brain below conscious access. Acquiring and improving such techniques may be undertaken consciously and determinedly, and yet the learning taking place is often in terms of processes to which the conscious brain has no direct access. This is learning-by-doing at its most extreme.

A different and more centralised mechanism may be at work in the extreme forms of learning-by-watching. Copying whole-body movements may in many cases draw on a process of mimesis in which subconscious processes map the actions which enable another observed person to carry out a particular activity and directly convert this into a programme of action for their own body. Self-observation may lead us to the conclusion that this is the kind of activity in which self-conscious reflection may be deleterious for the success of the underlying mechanism.

It is apparent that sport and entertainment, activities of the military, emergency and medical services, and driving and flying, particularly in passenger transport, are all activities in which action faster than conscious thought will often be demanded. We need to consider the fine distinctions between action completely without thought, as in reflex actions, actions which react to feedback which is itself faster than conscious thought, as in the hammering example, and action which needs to react faster than conscious thought to exigencies or conditions which initially have to be consciously learned but which must subsequently act as triggers. This leads to situating the actions within context-dependent memory and the priming effect of environments and familiar action patterns.

It is then necessary to consider whether it is possible to distinguish this kind of action faster than thought from the acquisition of habits, such as those of workers on an assembly line, which can become both automatic and stereotyped so that conscious thought appears to play no ongoing role.

We should also consider the possibility that the speed of thought is not always the critical factor, and that there are some bodily mechanisms which can be made more or less automatic more easily than others because they take advantage of innate mechanisms of balance and inertia in movement.

Routines and habits

Nelson and Winter (1982, pp. 99–136; and see our discussion in Chapter 5 of this volume) identify routines as the basic building blocks of business, a finding which is obviously applicable to other forms of organisation. Routines are combinations of habits (used here again in the colloquial sense), and conversely they provide the environment within which habits can develop. We all know that we are less habit-bound when we leave the environments which provide the normal supports and cues for our habits. Habits are useful because we know that they work for us, but there is a serious possibility that they may be sub-optimal. When we are put into a new environment, there is a period of experimentation after which we settle down into new habits. Habits have the obvious virtue that we do not expend mental energy on discovery and experimentation. A hidden value which is thrown into perspective by Polanyi is that we will build up a fund of knowledge in the form of expectations of what normally happens which will make us sensitive to quite small variations and their possible influence on our intentions.

Whether a routine, a particular set of habits shared by a group of co-operating individuals, is sub-optimal is very difficult to establish, since to do so would require systematically varying all of the many variable factors in the routine as a whole. In her pioneering – but, by the nature of the task, very limited – exploration of the problematic opened by Nelson and Winter, Ambrosini felt constrained to concentrate on behaviours which were judged by participants to have a positive effect on the competitive advantage, that is to say on the performance, of the firm. The tacit routines which were not so judged were not investigated (Ambrosini 2003; see also Ambrosini and Bowman 2001).

Habits involve both motor mechanisms – even if this means only walking a particular path – and knowledge, even if this means only passing on a delivery to a particular person. They could be important for the investigation of the underlying mechanisms of the tacit component of all knowledge and skill precisely because they can be embodied in procedures simpler than the procedures of a doctor or a pilot. They are also central to a routine, because every routine means that the same things should happen time after time. The tacit component involved in every activity has a lot to do with whether the routine includes what to do when things do not turn out the way they are expected to. The balance between routinisation and improvisation is dependent on what team members do or do not know about the wider context and environment of their normal activities. This brings us to the question of explicit communication.

Tacit knowing and the dynamic of subsidiary and focal awareness

Polanyi considers all knowledge to be activated only in the undertaking of some achievement or discovery. Our aims dictate the kinds of processes we will use, and in doing so we will activate to a greater or lesser extent all of the mechanisms which we have learned to associate with the processes in hand. Some of these processes may have been learned implicitly, and some of them may need to be exercised implicitly. Some of them may have been learned tacitly, and some of them may be of the kind which imposes tacitness in their use. Others may have initially been learned as verbal or written instructions, but in use their exact details will have been interpreted and perhaps revised in the light of experience, which may itself involve implicit and tacit elements of learning. Cutting across this we have the dynamic of focal and subsidiary awareness. Our focal awareness may be centred on something of which we have full explicit knowledge, or it may be centred on a problem or a crisis of which we have only a hazy idea. So the degree of our familiarity with the focal item does not necessarily correspond with the degree of implicitness or tacitness of the body of knowledge and experience which we bring to bear on it.

We therefore propose that it is necessary to use two scales, one of which will characterise the implicit, tacit or explicit (this category itself still needs to be analysed in more detail) nature of the knowledge or skill which we bring to bear on the problem. The other is the degree of the implicitness, tacitness or explicitness inherent in the problem which is posed to our focal awareness.

It is also necessary to remember that the holding, learning, interpretation and communication of clear and distinct ideas appear to require the activation of large amounts of implicit knowledge; in other words, all use of explicit knowledge rests on the activation of an 'iceberg' of implicit and tacit knowledge and skill, while the reverse is not the case. This is the intrusion into every use of knowledge and skill of the fact that the implicit and tacit are evolutionarily older and that explicit processes rely on a multitude of activities which either cannot or cannot simultaneously be made conscious.

We must further recall that all processes will activate a penumbra of associated processes, some priming us to be fluently able to process the specific kinds of information relevant to the specific process at hand, others mapping out the pathways which our decisions or the feedback from the process itself might dictate. The extent of these processes will be different in different cases, and this may be inherent in the relatively simple or complicated nature of the task, or it may reflect only the limitations of our personal knowledge of the matter.

The underlying reality may therefore be diagrammatically represented:

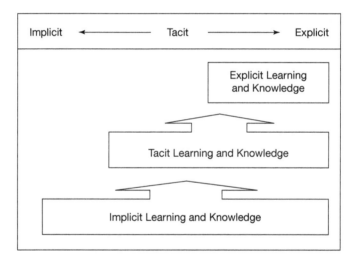

When we move on to look at tacit knowledge, we must realise that the distinction between implicit and explicit knowledge is effaced and replaced by the distinctions of focal and subsidiary awareness relevant to the particular stage of the particular process which is taking place. Diagrammatically this is shown at the top of the opposite page.

While this is the major trend, it must also be remembered that the use of knowledge in action also requires the backgrounding or making subsidiary of much explicit knowledge, possibly including the explicit instructions through which we first learned how to carry out the action question, so that we arrive at the diagram at the foot of the opposite page.

Above a certain, as yet unclear, threshold, the focus of our focal awareness can be located anywhere on the scale from implicit to explicit knowledge, and draws on the background input from both more explicit and less explicit sources of knowledge. The focus of focal awareness should not be identified with the

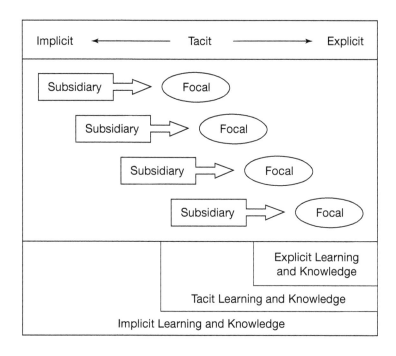

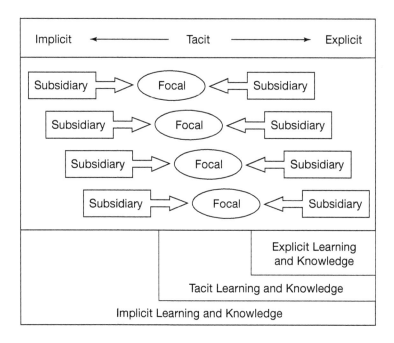

arena in which we use clear and distinct ideas. Rather, it is whatever we actually need to focus on, and we have no control over how clear our ideas of it may be. We can be just as focused in following a hunch or in doing what 'seems right' as in using a clearly and distinctly worked-out plan.

Therefore, the mapping of the activation of implicit, tacit and explicit elements of skill during a process aimed at a goal will never be static but is constantly changing as the achievement of sub-goals makes certain outcomes and alternative pathways less relevant and calls on the activation of other pathways and alternatives for further stages.

We should also recognise that we should not start from the paradigm of the manufacture of objects according to a preconceived plan or template. The majority of human activity starts from goals which are more qualitative and which can undergo evolution during their execution.

Multiple forms of explicit communication – pros and cons

We now need to discuss the process of making knowledge explicit. There are many aspects of my everyday life and surroundings which I have never consciously thought about before but which I could nevertheless easily explain to a foreigner, a novice or an investigator. But here we must draw a distinction between my own tacit, implicit and explicit knowledge. When I describe a journey, I mostly do not know whether I am telling someone to take the third left-hand turning from discrete memory, from logical implication, or by 'walking through' the journey in my mind. Depending on my personal preferences and the way in which I myself originally learned the information, I may be doing all of these in different combinations. When I exercise my own tacit knowledge of the journey, I call on all of these more or less implicit or explicit resources to do so. If someone else once makes the journey on the basis of what I have told them, they begin to build up a tacit knowledge of the journey with a different and dynamic mixture of clues. We say that someone knows how to make the journey if they have successfully done so a number of times. In Polanyi's terms the tacit knowing of the journey which they exhibit is a mixture of a focal awareness of the goal and an ability to call on a stock of elements in subsidiary awareness which suffice to proceed towards the goal. Although there is no way of pronouncing that their tacit knowledge is the 'same' as mine, we have both developed a capability of using a stock of knowledge which 'works for us'.

If we want to make the tacit knowledge of the journey explicit, we can quite easily do so. But if we give a list of turnings, we will find that some people will find this more useful than others. If we supplement this with a map, we will help more people. Others may prefer a written narrative or a verbal account. Yet others may benefit from adding landmarks to the bare description of the route. By adding to our modalities of communication, we ensure that more people can successfully build up the capability, but we no longer know which channel of 'explicit' information they are using to do so. Discrepancies can arise between the information presented in different modes. Within an apprenticeship these discrepancies can be ironed out. If we turn our sets of instructions and maps into a manual to be used 'cold' by novices, we are making assumptions about their literacy, numeracy, map-reading and cultural references which may not be borne out. The interpretation of 'explicit' knowledge is itself a capability in the exercise of which tacit knowing draws on a variety of implicitly and explicitly learned components.

What comprises explicit knowledge?

Tacit knowledge has been discussed within management theory in contrast with explicit knowledge. In this context, explicit knowledge is usually itself underdefined. If we look at an organisation from the top down, we can expect to find some legal documents containing a definition of the purpose of the organisation and the distribution of legal responsibilities within it. There will be documentation of the ownership or renting of buildings, vehicles and machinery; insurance policies; lists and diagrams of the posts within the organisation and their holders, and the division of responsibilities. For each such post or class of posts there may be a job description, which in turn will refer to the need to consult manuals for the materials, vehicles, machinery and tools normally in use, and for their maintenance. There will be legally required instructions for maintaining a safe environment. The organisation may hold or license patents and may also have some recipes which it prefers to keep confidential rather than patent. So ostensibly the organisation has a body of explicit knowledge which describes what it does and how it does it in such a way that reading these documents would allow a newcomer to begin to participate in its activities in a meaningful and useful way, or to investigate problems. If we look at explicit knowledge from the bottom up, we could find that a starter in the organisation is immediately confronted with a highly signed environment, with a wide range of traffic and safety signage, departmental and personal nameplates, and maps and diagrams of work procedures and flows. We need to ask: how do these masses of texts and signs become knowledge? This obviously takes place only when they are read, and specifically only when they are read and understood, and only when they are read and understood as relevant to a particular context.

Explicit knowledge is thus always specific to the ability and habituation of the user to acquire and absorb information from the media used. This generally requires literacy, in one specific language, and even when signage is designed so as not to require literacy, much signage still assumes a basic familiarity with some conventions of signage itself. However, speaking and reading a language are actually an insufficient basis for understanding most of the explicit knowledge that is available. It would be prohibitively expensive to describe the use of every technology in the world as if the prospective user were a complete beginner. Therefore, most formulations of explicit knowledge are aimed at a reader who has a particular professional background. It could be said that these users are primed by their previous exposure to a given body of professional explicit knowledge, as formulated in the relevant textbooks. Their absorption of knowledge would thus be all of a kind, although spread over different locales and times. The documents seen later contain an implicit cross-reference to the more introductory documents in the field. This assumption of an axiomatic basis for knowledge which is subsequently deduced from general principles would be begging the question of exactly how people learn skills.

A completely different approach to explicit knowledge would be the following: most documentation is not intended to be educational, but regulatory. Ignorance of the law is no excuse, and a very large part of the explicit knowledge formulated within an organisation is telling people what they must do, and how they must do it, in order for the organisation as a whole to comply with various legal and insurance imperatives. How people actually learn this knowledge and acquire the relevant habits is another matter.

At the other extreme there are some job descriptions which are genuinely intended to tell an incoming worker what their job consists of. These are written by old incumbents or by supervisors who know what is done on a day-to-day basis. Reading such documents, it is immediately clear which tasks are taken to be obvious to persons entering the post from a broadly similar work back-ground. Such job descriptions list which tasks are done at which times of day, on which days of the month, where inputs come from and where outputs go, and who to consult with problems, while leaving the description of what takes place almost completely to the imagination of the reader. These kinds of job descriptions are regarded as useful because they help the worker plan their days, but to the outsider they communicate very little.

In contrast to this there are highly developed competency systems which use weekly or monthly reviews to chart an employee's productivity, performance and development, based on discussion of data from output levels, self-reporting, supervision and external sources of training. These would seem to provide a constant stream of highly explicit knowledge about what is being done, by whom, and at what levels of attainment and quality. Against this, there is dissatisfaction among large organisations with the results of generic competency systems, and a correlated tendency to tweak the system to match more closely the patterns of work within the organisation, or to develop a completely in-house competency system in tandem with the development of proprietorial production and product development systems. The explicit knowledge gen-erated by the system therefore tends to revert to an in-house jargon which in turn becomes the preserve of specialists within the organisation, who also develop expertise in interpreting the 'real' significance of trends and problems within the system.[7]

What is knowledge? What is communication? Implicit learning, tacit knowledge and distributed cognition

This topic can be related to the question of knowing-how and knowing-who. It is a commonplace that knowledge of people and of what they can or cannot do is as important as, or more important than, what each individual knows how to do themself. It may be that much of this knowledge is itself implicit and in turn concerns knowledge about the knowledge of others which is also implicit. This throws a new light on the importance of Granovetter's embeddedness and on 'insider' knowledge of networks, markets and bureaucracies. Nelson and Winter define routines as the actions of teams within which each member knows what to do, where to get inputs, where to pass on outputs, who to go to with problems, as well as knowing their own 'technical' tasks (see Chapter 5).

All complex human organisations are characterised by the existence of shared, distributed tacit knowledge (see Salomon 1993). This is knowledge which depends on particular channels of communication or particular assignments of responsibility. It is a function of the division of labour but this must be understood to be itself a compromise between technological constraints and systems of governance. The exact demarcations between the roles of different individuals may be specific to a particular team and a particular environment, and may be tacit knowledge in Boisot's third sense that no one has ever asked themself why it is done in this particular way. Individuals within teams and groups evolve ways of distributing tasks in line with their particular experience, skills and preferences, and these distributions then mould the further evolution of skills within the group. Groups which have evolved a different pattern of distribution of tasks will not necessarily be able to evaluate the stage of development of a task begun by a different group.

Implicit learning, tacit knowing and explicit knowledge versus information, data, meaning, knowledge and understanding

The foregoing explanations of the concepts of tacit knowing and implicit learning will have begun to make clear that knowledge cannot be cleanly categorised into different mutually exclusive classes or categories, but that knowledge-in-use must be investigated and analysed in terms of the differential balance of various components. There is implicit learning of correlations and patterns in reality which may or may not be duplicated by explicit knowledge of the same phenomena. When these phenomena are manipulated or diagnosed in practice, both the implicit and the explicit resources of the individual may be called upon and contribute to the outcome. Likewise there are manipulative or whole-body actions which are learned implicitly, that is to say by trial and error or by watching and copying the actions of others. It may be possible to describe these actions in words, but if the recitation of this verbal description takes more time than the action itself it cannot be useful and may be a distraction if called on during the execution of the action. However, mentoring by experts who are able to analyse the actions of a learner and give them hints or clues, or even simply to tell them when they are getting it right and when not, can contribute to successful outcomes, and this knowledge must be explicit from the mentor's point of view even if the learner will not reach the same stage of reflection until much later, after having mastered the process. There are some actions, however, which exceed the speed of thought and which can only be acquired as habits. These may involve the interpretation of feedback, as when we interpret whether a nail is being hammered in straight. There is a trade-off here because it might seem that we should simply hammer more slowly in order to aim more precisely each time, but this could lead to a loss of the information from the feedback and a greater number of false aims. The first hit provides rapidly fading knowledge about the correct trajectory in the context of the specific texture of the site. It may therefore be necessary to allow this kind of action to become implicit even when it might seem not absolutely necessary to do so.

We do not know the real balance of usefulness between relying on implicit knowledge when explicit knowledge is also available. This is because implicit processes are more instinctive and may therefore be more robust against distraction and against the false identification of contexts. They would also be more resistant to purely verbal confusion. Research on these problems can proceed only when the problems are seen and formulated as such.

Polanyi's theory suggests that tacit knowing will be the mode in which 'knowledge' from both implicit and explicit sources will be subliminally mobilised in subsidiary awareness to support actions being carried out in focal awareness. The phrase 'focal awareness' has no necessary implications for the extent to which the individual has a clear idea of what the object of focal attention is. It may be a 'problem' or an unidentified phenomenon. In regard to tacit knowing, the words 'implicit', 'explicit' and 'tacit' are not permanently attached to any particular item of knowledge but are functions of the role which knowledge plays in any particular pattern of focal and subsidiary awareness. At the same time, it is necessary to bear in mind that the products of implicit learning are not deleted when the 'same' knowledge is consciously acquired, and that, depending on patterns of use, the consciously and unconsciously acquired versions of the knowledge may be differentially activated and updated.

Information and data

Information and data are both terms which are used in information theory. 'Data' is used more or less in its vernacular meaning, a collection of data being a collection of facts, each an individual 'datum', such as the value of a particular variable in regard to a particular individual at a particular time. Data can only exist within a defined 'ontology' which prescribes what kind of 'objects' can or cannot have particular variables assigned to them and what the value range of these variables for these objects can be. 'Information' is used technically in a way which is confusing to outsiders since it is applied to the method of coding of the 'data' rather than to its 'content' as normally understood. At present the predominant method is the use of binary code, the reduction of all input to numbers which are expressed in the binary code, which uses only 0 and 1. Music and pictures are currently being stored and distributed in binary ('digital') form, their quality being assured by the use of a range of values which surpasses that of the range perceptible to the human eye and ear – supposedly, although this is disputed by some connoisseurs. It is unclear at present whether this is merely an artefact of the recognition of the absence of the 'interference' which was previously ubiquitous in recorded sound, or whether some individuals have highly developed mechanisms of parsing or sampling sound which may give music a flavour which they find has been obliterated in digitised recordings.

However this may be, we do not currently know the means by which information in the technical sense of information theory is stored in the brain; nor do we know the limits, if any, of the 'ontologies' which are – or which can, or indeed cannot, be – encoded in the brain. We are at the stage of only being able to access individual items of 'data' from the human brain or mind. The individuals concerned may themselves believe that their knowledge is in the form of an 'ontology' which is that of the (religious, philosophical, scientific or cultural) belief system to which they belong or subscribe, but this assumption is often found to be contradicted by reality. Modern science is a social system specifically addressed to ensuring an identity of 'ontology' in this technical sense. Polanyi was an enthusiastic member of this community who emphasised the need to accept a discipline which sometimes rejects correct intuitions because they are not substantiated in the correct form, just as a legal system must accept the guilty sometimes going unpunished if technicalities are not observed. He only objected to the identification of the specific historically arrived-at stage of this 'ontology' with the whole of reality.[8]

It is in this context that we progress to the transition from data to meaning. It is only contexts, and ultimately values and goals, which give meaning to any particular data. Dead facts, which have no significance, are difficult to remember for this very reason. Just as scientists and doctors are able to build up 'gestalten' from abstract patterns because they have been trained to see their significance, so 'dry' facts come alive when they are part of the dynamic of a business, a law case, a diagnosis or a battle. The proliferation of 'dead facts' is more properly a proliferation of specialised contexts and occupations, within which these facts come alive, but only for a shrinkingly small number of experts and specialists. Within these contexts, in turn, meaningful data becomes knowledge when it is unified in a framework of relevance. The unity of knowledge and action, like that of 'knowing how and knowing that', is driven by goals and the expert ability to achieve such goals and to judge how movement towards them is progressing. Conversely, as illustrated above by Polanyi's comment about a map, new arrangements of data may give rise to unexpected new insights about their significance.

Understanding is also a question of the integration of knowledge, skills and meaning into goal-oriented activity. When some people say that others do not 'understand' a subject matter although they know the facts and can operate the procedures, it is this integration of skills and knowledge into an orientation to a goal, or at least the lack of integration in orientation towards a shared goal, which is experienced as lacking. Polanyi helps us to see why this is the case with his concepts of the tacit dynamic, the way in which scientific theories and other systems of thought are not merely passively resting on a body of tacit knowing, which is simply subservient to the declared aims of conscious thought, but structure and channel the dynamic towards goals which may not be explicitly grasped or held. The structure of this dynamic also does not cease with the attainment of any stated goal but leads us to see further possibilities and opportunities, so that discordant structures of tacit assumptions will lead different individuals and groups to see the dynamics of developments moving in different directions. Yet in contrast to the positivist programme, Polanyi does not believe that such discrepancy can ever be completely removed by the discovery of an objective lowest common denominator on which we can all agree. At the same time he also does not resign to relativism or solipsism. He sees the scientific community as a forum for convergence through shared processes of discovery towards growing agreement on what is jointly experienced, while accepting that this activity is carried out by individuals who embody tacit assumptions which lead them to interpret and develop this body of ideas in different ways.

The tacit component of all knowledge and skill

Throughout human life there is a real and an institutional distinction between knowledge and skill. This is valid, since it reflects the different ways in which such things can paradigmatically be tested and displayed, knowledge being more easily displayed by verbalisation or writing, and skills requiring real contexts and usually some artefacts and materials. If it is once conceded that skills and knowledge are a continuum, with all skills involving some knowledge and all knowledge involving some skill, there is a tendency to identify tacit knowledge with the grey area in the middle of this continuum, or else to suppose that it consists of that unconceptualised knowledge which is hidden within the body of skills. Hopefully the reader will by now have grasped that this is a misconceptualisation of the role of tacit knowing. The model of focal and subsidiary awareness leads Polanyi to see the tacitness of knowledge as a variable of any particular situation. It is less misleading to speak of tacit knowing rather than tacit knowledge, but this begs the question: knowing what? The answer to this is that the object of tacit knowing is the tacit coefficient of all skilled action and thus inclusive of the use of explicit or codified knowledge, which must always be contextualised and decoded in appropriate skilful ways.

There is thus no distinctly identifiable body of tacit knowledge, but rather tacit knowing summates for each and every particular situation of application all of the background inputs to the focally attended-to process. Among these are:

1   the motor-body habits which have been developed, some of which may be practised at speeds more rapid than the conscious mind can grasp;
2   the tricks and knacks which have been learned from experience, many of which may be unthought-out or may be beyond the power of the skilled person to explain;
3   the entire background knowledge of what can go wrong and what to do about it in each case, which may be 'known' in an explicit codified form, but which cannot be consulted in this form in the relevant time parameter and therefore must take the form of a pattern of possible pathways within which the person can orient themself; likewise
4   the recognition of physiognomies of symptoms and signals, which again can be known on one level completely explicitly but which must be accessed instinctively in use; and
5   a wider grasp of the relative importance of the process in hand relative to other events which may intrude on the person while executing it.

All of these things may exist in the form of codified explicit knowledge and the person may have passed examinations on this knowledge, but their skill depends on being able to call on a pattern of clues, signals and symptoms in action. In some professions there may be processes of training which bring about a fusion of the codified and the instinctive forms of the same 'body' of knowledge; in many it must be admitted that formal learning has to be supplemented by practice before this fusion takes place, and there is always the possibility that formal and practical learning will diverge. This is particularly a problem wherever the apprenticeship model of education and training is replaced by formal schooling, and also wherever technical change outstrips the capacity of educational and training systems or is isolated from it by spatial or institutional distance.

The implication is that, first, the 'tacit component' of all skilled tasks must be mapped without any preconceptions as to whether a task is high-skilled or low-skilled, or even without drawing distinctions between the 'tasks' of a situation and the necessary 'background' knowledge, which may all be different in reality from as described within systems and organisation maps. Second, the specific forms of the learning or acquisition of this tacit component must be determined without preconceptions as to the value of any particular model of training. Third, it must be accepted that the resulting model will remain fluid because technology and ways of working are increasingly subject to change.

We have thus moved from the concept of tacit knowledge, which is too easily misunderstood as a body of knowledge alongside explicit knowledge, through that of tacit knowing, which is better, but still may be taken to imply a special kind of knowing with a special subject matter, to the tacit component, which may more adequately express the situational aspect of subsidiary awareness in subordination to a shifting pattern of focal awareness. Some of the elements of the tacit component are inherently implicit or tacit, others only accidentally so; some are not necessarily tacit at all but become so only when they are backgrounded in particular schemes of the focal–subsidiary balance.

The tacit component must now be seen on two levels. One is whether the tacit component in use in a particular situation is itself optimal for that situation. Systems may not work because of an absent tacit component. This was the case in Polanyi's example of the light-bulb factory, and in the power-generation example of Sapphire studied by Collins.[9] The other level is that the processes currently in use themselves may not be optimal. This in turn gives rise to two further possibilities. Where a sub-optimal system is in use, a tacit component may evolve which compensates for the deficiencies of the system as designed. If this is discovered to be the case, it is an open question whether this should lead to trying to make the original design work or to accept the subverted but operative system as adequate.

Beyond this we lack any data to begin to explore the question of the optimality of the tacit component in different contexts, or how to induct new individuals into improved patterns of tacit components. This is part of the wider problem that organisations with idiosyncratic systems are often aware of a lack of skills among their workers, but are unable to identify sources of specific training. They try out a series of available courses and hope that some useful elements will emerge from different sources.

This leads us to the question of the value of clustering. In rapidly evolving sectors, tacit knowledge cannot be mediated by the institutions of initial training, and some degree of diffusion and sharing of new tacit knowledge within sectors is required. In order for this to take place, there must be some incentive to share knowledge with competitors. The following chapters review the literature on innovation, innovation sharing, knowledge diffusion and the competitive advantage of clustering in order to situate the possible models of tacit knowledge diffusion in this context.

A provisional proposal

A first approximation to mapping the tacit component of any competency would be to progress from the necessarily implicit levels through the necessarily tacit, optionally tacit, optionally explicit and necessarily explicit levels. A crude list might be as follows:

- necessarily implicit movements (movements faster than conscious control);

- implicit decision processes ('instinctive' decisions or guesses);
- trained implicit movements and actions (secondary 'instinctive' actions);
- necessarily tacit actions (actions which inhibit speech and/or reflection);
- tacit decision processes (decisions concerning processes never articulated);
- actions learned though mimesis;
- actions learned by doing;
- secondarily tacit actions (originally learned by explicit instruction);
- actions and decisions guided by explicit thought;
- actions and decisions guided by explicit conversation and co-operation;
- actions and decisions guided by explicit logical reasoning.

The presence or absence, extent and contribution to critical outcomes of these different components would provide an initial mapping of the tacit component.

However, we must recall that it is not only the active use of skill or knowledge which has degrees of tacitness. The nature of the problem itself may present different levels of clarity which require a response on their own level. We can therefore consider asking for a ranking in terms of questions such as these:

- Is the problem as initially grasped fully explicit?
- If not, is it the nature or only the extent of the problem which remains unclear?
- Is the nature of the response given, or will it depend on the investigation of the nature of the problem?

Another aspect which must be considered is that of the extent of the branching pathways which may be involved. This brings us directly to the unity of skill and knowledge in action, as the recognition of specific physiognomies may be the points at which pathways branch. It may be necessary to bring in the question of what level of physiognomic judgement is required; whether, in terms of the medical example discussed above, the practitioner must begin from the normal physiognomy and notice pathological deviations from this, or go further to recognise the typical physiognomies of specific pathologies and work from there. This could be formulated as follows in terms of whether the work:

- consists of one-to-one matchings or choosing between more complex pathways;
- can be immediately decided or requires tests;
- is directly turned into action or leads to referrals or planning.

This is only a first approximation to what would be required. We need to remember that while some of these questions may seem to be identical with existing descriptions of competencies, we are interested in finding out at each level the activation patterns which are produced by the situation and the way in which they change through different stages of the process. This means investigating the balance between, and possibly the conflict between, the inputs from implicit, tacit and explicit resources, and the extent to which each plays a role at different times.

The natural home for this approach would be existing systems of competency mapping, competency management and personal development. Our interest in 'tacit knowledge' as discussed in the wider management and organisation literature originally arose from the study of such systems and the possibilities of improving them (Cullen, Jones and Miller 2001). An advantage of using this approach is that national systems which have adopted the competency approach to skills and which have carried out a reclassification of their occupational profiles on this basis will also have systems of expert appraisal of the relevance of competencies to achieving successful critical outcomes. This would be the best approach to take further in the mapping and criticality assessment of the implicit and tacit components of competencies.

Techniques of mapping distribution and diffusion of tacit knowledge in organisations

We have found that development on mapping tacit knowledge for the purposes of diffusion of tacit knowledge as such without any aspirations to convert it into anything else has been taken furthest by the work of Busch, Richards and Dampney.[10] The outcome of their investigations up to now has been two-fold. On the one hand, the authors have produced a damning judgement on the concepts of capture, articulation, conversion and circulation of tacit knowledge within organisations on the models of Nonaka and his associates. In the abstract to Busch and Richards (n.d.c) they draw the conclusion that 'the optimal organization for tacit knowledge transfer contains highly interconnected social human networks and is minimally reliant on the use of technology for communication'. On the other hand, they are very positive about the possibilities of mapping the presence of personal tacit knowledge and of producing visual maps of the presence of tacit knowledge within organisations in order to avoid the development of bottlenecks which might arise because of lack of communication and contact between different parts and levels of the organisation.

Busch and Richards' *Acquisition of Articulable Tacit Knowledge* (2004) develops a cyclical model of how the codification of tacit knowledge always gives rise to new layers of tacit knowledge. Systems, technologies and work practices give rise to tacit knowledge, parts of which may eventually become codified. We use their terminology despite the recognition that explicit knowledge is not a conversion of tacit knowledge but only a guide to it. The new tacit knowledge generated should not be seen as confined to the use of the codified knowledge itself, although this can also happen, but is rather the result of drawing the implications of knowledge once it becomes codified. This is particularly relevant to growing organisations.

The authors are particularly interested in diffusion of the knowledge of experts. They realise that the expert is not always the senior figure, hence they concentrate on the situation of the older senior figure who acquires knowledge of new technologies from younger junior figures, perhaps overlooking the transfer of knowledge from older, less qualified experts to younger, more highly qualified and nominally senior figures. They suggest the need for mentoring as a channel for the transmission of tacit knowledge. It is at this point that they mention the negative effect of telecommuting on the transfer of tacit knowledge. They note that much work on tacit knowledge capture is posited on the need to formalise and so hopefully generalise expert problem-solving methods. It may be relevant to refer to the literature on expertise cited earlier (Patel and Groen 1991), which suggests that expert problem-solving uses different gestalts from novice problem-solving because experts work from their acquired stock of physiognomies of problems while novices work from the paradigm state and attempt to identify problems on a checklist approach. This may be a problem for any approach which assumes that problem-solving solutions are themselves 'learnable' without the underlying range of experience.

This problem becomes relevant when the authors explain that they are using a system based on Wagner and Sternberg's TKIM. This system is a test of how expert individuals are. The original TKIM was based on summing the judgements of dozens of experts. The test version is then intended to discover to what extent juniors have acquired the general body of tacit knowledge of the organisation. The extent to which they have done so is also an indicator of their ability to uncover the tacit knowledge of any organisation they might be in. The TKIM does not make allowance for the possibility that the tacit knowledge of junior and senior members may be of a different kind. Therefore, when Busch and Richards propose using this framework as a tool for elicitation of expert status as perceived by colleagues, they may risk fudging the different methods by which experts and novices reach their conclusions.

This does not affect the general conclusions of the paper, which were that small organisations were best for diffusion of tacit knowledge while larger ones had bottlenecks indicating that some colleagues were not part of the knowledge-sharing pool either as individuals or because they were ghettoised in a small clique which did not share knowledge with the wider organisation.

Four papers by this team of authors (Busch and Richards n.d.a and b; Busch, Richards and Dampney 2001b and 2003) describe different aspects of the methodology and modelling techniques used in their research. Busch and Richards (n.d.a) describes the adaptation of the Sternberg TKIM method to the information systems context and the use of the data to map the status of experts. In a first procedure, experts were nominated by their colleagues. The answers given by this group were therefore classed as 'expert answers'. The experimenters were able to identify a group of 'expert non-experts'; that is, individuals whose answers were as good as those of the experts but who were not identified by their colleagues as experts. This group was seen by the researchers as presenting a problem of knowledge diffusion in that colleagues would not normally approach them for expert advice and therefore their knowledge resources would be underused. It would therefore be of particular interest to discover if these individuals were members of groups which were marginalised within the wider social networks or whether they were personally failing to display their knowledge. Busch and Richards (n.d.b) uses the language use of individuals as a proxy for their ethnic background and uses social network analysis to discover if ethnic minority groups have a tendency to be isolated from wider social networks. This was found to be a problem with possible bottleneck effects on the diffusion of tacit knowledge only in the largest of the three organisations investigated. Busch, Richards and Dampney (2001b) and (2003) present the methodology of the visual mapping of distribution of tacit knowledge within organisations. The methodology was tested in a pilot site where the results indicated that one individual was a key figure in mediating between two groups who networked intensely among themselves but were otherwise quite separate. This was a 'gatekeeper' person who was also explicitly identified as a mediator of knowledge within the organisation.

This research was undertaken by a group who have seen many of the inadequacies of the prevailing discourse on 'tacit knowledge'. Their approach is not developed to contribute directly to the problem of creating a taxonomy of the tacit component, but it could be a valuable contribution to mapping and understanding the dynamics of the spread of tacit knowledge associated with innovations and the use of new processes, equipment and materials. Their methodology is demonstrated within discrete organisations, but it could also be extended to the diffusion of skills along the value and supply chain or between research and development or joint project partners.

The USDOL O*NET Content Model

The Occupational Information Network, or O*NET, as well as other national models derived from similar methodologies, might provide opportunities for situating a mapping of the tacit component of skills and knowledge. The O*NET was developed by the United States Department of Labor in the 1990s as a replacement for the Dictionary of Occupational Titles (see Peterson *et al.* 1995, 1999, 2001, and Converse *et al.* 2004). The principal novelty of the new development was the application to the old DOT occupations and a range of newly evolving occupations of a universal system of descriptors of the requirements of jobs (see Table 4.1). This system of descriptors was designed to capture cross-job and cross-occupational descriptors in order to facilitate both labour mobility and the emergence of generic elements of education and training which would have cross-occupational relevance. The majority of descriptors have three parameters: the level of the task or ability required in the job; the importance of the task to the job; and the frequency of the occurrence of the task on the job. Similar systems of occupational profiling using cross-

Table 4.1 O*NET job requirement descriptor categories

1 Worker requirements	Skills Knowledge Education
2 Occupational requirements	Generalised work activities Work content Organisational content
3 Experience requirements	—
4 Worker characteristics	Abilities Occupational values and interests Work styles
5 Occupational characteristics	—
6 Occupation-specific requirements	—

occupational descriptors have been developed in Australasia and South Africa, and are in progress in Europe under the aegis of EURES (the European Employment Service).

The system of skills, knowledge, work activity and ability descriptors used in the O*NET and similar public systems provides an accessible and widely used framework which could be a template for the mapping of the tacit and implicit component. Using this starting point makes clear that 'tacit knowledge' is not a new kind of knowledge alongside other kinds of skill and knowledge but is an underlying element in the acquisition and use of all kinds of skill. It would also facilitate the mapping of the tacit component of specific competencies which might need to be diffused in tandem with the diffusion of new technologies or with the use of new equipment and materials.

Mapping is not conversion

We have outlined a possible project of the mapping of the tacit component of the skills and knowledge used in particular competencies, as an aid to the diffusion of these competencies. We must stress that this is not equivalent to making the 'tacit knowledge' actually embodied and used in these competencies 'explicit'. Learning-by-watching, guided learning-by-doing, and learning assisted by illustrated manuals, videos or virtual walkthroughs are all forms of induction. All skills are ultimately learned either by induction or by learning-by-doing, and all explicit instructions are only aids to accelerate the process of learning-by-doing. The process of mapping the structure and elements of tacit knowing associated with particular skills is one of many processes which help to ensure the success of diffusion of competencies by aiding the induction process. When fully developed, an analysis of the tacit component may also suggest ways of strengthening the competency by replacing or supplementing one form of tacit skills by another. Analysis of skills does not 'destroy' the tacitness of the tacit component when actually used, but also should not be seen as a 'conversion' of one kind of knowledge into another. Learning, having and using skills is one thing, and talking about them and understanding why and how they work is another.

Most tacit knowledge will remain tacit, and new tacit knowledge is generated very rapidly. Attempts to produce manuals of the tacit knowledge of an organisation can rapidly become compendiums without reaching the goal of being able to communicate those elements that really enable success. Personal contact, preferably face to face, or, if mediated by ICTs, on the basis of a background of shared contact and experience enabling easy communication through a common task-related language, has been identified as the only way to transmit tacit knowledge and skills.[11] In large organisations this kind of contact and transmission cannot be taken for granted but must be fostered by the organisation and its networks. Part of this process will be the mapping of the presence of tacit knowledge and the validation of 'experts' and 'gurus' who are sources of the best tacit knowledge. We have reverted here to the terminology of 'tacit knowledge' because we are referring to the personal characteristics of individuals rather than to the components of skills. We must talk about the tacit components of a skill, a competency, a routine or a complete process of production, but the term 'tacit knowledge' may perhaps usefully be used to refer to the cross-section of such knowledge acquired by any particular individual.

5 The real and false relevance of economic innovation

Schumpeter and innovation as the only source of growth

Why did we begin a discussion of the relevance of tacit knowing with a review of theories of competition? We could have begun directly by investigating the different kinds of tacit knowing found in different contexts and worked towards a taxonomy and a mapping of the components of the tacit component in time and on different levels of time and sectoral or cultural space. Instead we are attempting to identify particularly interesting problems around which to organise our investigations. As Nelson and Winter (1982, p. 134) state:

> Theorists should aim to tell the truth in their theorizing, but they cannot aim to tell the whole truth. For to theorize is precisely to focus on those entities and relationships in reality that are believed to be central to the phenomena observed – and largely to ignore the rest. To advance a new theory is to propose a shift of focus, to recognize as central considerations that were previously ignored.

This formulation itself perhaps betrays some influence of Polanyi's ideas on the authors. But our own focus is based on the following assumptions about exactly which phenomena are 'central' here, namely:

1 Tacit knowing and tacit inference as understood by Polanyi contain implications which have largely been overlooked by economic thinkers.
2 This is especially important for the activity of the entrepreneur specifically as understood by Schumpeter.
3 This has significant implications for Schumpeter's theory of creative destruction, especially in an informational interpretation of this process.

Theories of competition are meant to be models of how competition works in reality, although they begin by making a whole raft of abstractions in order to focus on specific aspects of reality (hopefully). We are picking up on this thread because we suppose that it might be possible to identify interesting patterns of association of different kinds of tacit knowing with the workings of different kinds of markets. This would be useful enough if it allowed us to map tacit components onto areas which appear to exemplify the workings of different kinds of market mechanisms in parallel through time; that is, in different sectoral or regional groupings. Schumpeter's theory of 'creative destruction', in its development through his lifetime, adds two extra twists to this, in that he first suggests that there is a mechanism which leads the nature of markets to change on a cyclical pattern, and later says that there might be some developments – essentially the 'industrialisation' of research and development – which could lead to a lessening of the power of these cycles. Finding out whether these cycles exist and, if so, whether their strength or frequency are really being affected by new developments would help us identify possible fields of application or opportunity for varying patterns of tacit knowing.

Schumpeter is also associated with a special theory of the importance of one particular kind of skills, those of the entrepreneur. In his early work Schumpeter makes a unique distinction between the skills of the entrepreneur and those of the inventor, the manager and the capitalist. Although any or all of these roles are often exercised by the same person, simultaneously or through time, Schumpeter alone has based his theory of the market and of profit and economic growth on drawing a very clear distinction between the capitalist and the entrepreneur. The former are the owners of capital who invest on the basis that they retain any surplus and bear any loss. Their skill is in the choice between different kinds and levels of risk. Entrepreneurs are those individuals who are capable both of seeing the possibility of what Schumpeter calls 'new combinations' and of making them into reality by organisation and intervention. These are, namely: new machinery, new working methods, new forms of work organisation, new sources of supply, new products to meet existing needs, new markets for existing products, new uses for existing products, new products which will create new needs.[1] Not all examples involve new technology in either the process or the product. Schumpeter sees a symbiotic relationship between capitalists and entrepreneurs as the fundamental characteristic of Western capitalist society: entrepreneurs have the vision which allows the constant discovery of new sources of profit (which however are soon eroded by 'normal' competition – Schumpeter 1961, p. 132), while the demand of entrepreneurs for speculative but essentially productive investment calls into existence the mechanism of banking and stock trading which ensures that all available individual surpluses are mobilised.

In his later works Schumpeter appeared to accept the inevitability of socialism on the basis that the work of the entrepreneur was being increasingly absorbed into the corporation in the form of institutionalised research and development. On the other hand, the work of the capitalist was itself, in a parallel process, being reduced to the decisions of banks or insurance societies, on the basis of their own institutionalised decision processes, to invest, directly or through the stock market, in one corporation rather than another. Schumpeter considered that these processes could lead to a lack of political will to maintain private capitalism. Some of his formulations suggested that the sources of technological innovation were themselves nearly exhausted.[2] He also appeared to concede that the institutionalisation of research and development could lead to a spreading out of the introduction of innovations, leading to reduction of the power of successive waves of creative destruction.[3]

We need to utilise these insights to begin to analyse changes in the patterns of skills, and particularly of the tacit, implicit and shared components of knowledge, in the areas of entrepreneurship and innovation. At the same time, we will try to identify some of the ways in which different patterns of market organisation and different ways of integrating the entrepreneurial activity will create and reward different kinds of tacit knowledge. We will mention and discuss a number of economic theories, but we shall not be attempting to innovate or even evaluate in these areas, but only to establish taxonomies in a new area of investigation. We are concerned with the area of skills. The kinds of distinctions and classifications which we are trying to establish concern the skills of economic creativity, leadership and innovation in the widest sense. These skills may be exhibited, under a fully developed division of labour and roles, as those of inventors, entrepreneurs, capitalists and managers. The skills of management may in turn be classified as those of the management of endogenous and exogenous change. Whether all of these skills will be embodied in separate persons and roles will depend on the wider systems of law and governance, patterns of the internal organisation of the firm, and the life-cycle of the individual firm.

Models of the market mechanism

We will first outline the distinction between Schumpeter's theory of creative destruction and other theories of market mechanisms, both equilibrium and non-equilibrium.

In the first instance we refer to the theory of general equilibrium. In its pure form this model abstracts from many features of the real world, such as imperfect competition, bounded rationality, the real costs of transactions and information, the institutionalisation of markets, and the ineradicability of ignorance and uncertainty. It nevertheless posits the real existence of a pattern of consumer preferences, which patterns of differential incentives lead producers to adapt to. Allowing for the fact that consumer preferences are a moving target, this gives adaptation a direction and thus allows a definition of fitness. We are not here concerned with the criticisms of what equilibrium theory leaves out or with various attempts to make its assumptions more realistic. Instead we take as a contrast the Austrian school, which posits that there is no pre-existing pattern of preferences to which entrepreneurial and competitive activity constitutes a path of approximation. The economy is a process in which preferences, needs, ends and means are always simultaneously undergoing redefinition.

Nevertheless, there are many regions of the real economy in which an approximation to the outcomes predicted by equilibrium theory may be found. These are generally areas such as raw materials, universal components, foodstuffs and some other basic commodities and services. These may be seen as markets within which it really is a question of meeting given needs with given means, while changes in factor supply, product demand and technological innovations can be seen as external disturbances to which the market rapidly and easily adapts. There have been many studies of the real working of competition to create more or less optimal equilibrium outcomes in these kinds of sectors. This will give rise to a situation where the premium skills and knowledge will be those of detailed familiarity with both existing technologies and market structures, and familiarity with the finely graded qualities of the commodity in question.[4] Within this context the diffusion and assimilation of innovations will generally leave a core of previous practices unchanged and will thus not seriously devalue the formal and tacit knowledges embodied in existing patterns of activity.

In contrast with this we can outline the Austrian model of entrepreneurial search as a model of a market which does not merely adapt to external disturbances. The task facing each individual entrepreneur is to find a new combination of economic factors which will succeed in a future situation that is not strictly predictable. This may be done by producing a new product, by using a new technology, or by combining inputs in a new way. The important factor is that all such new undertakings are essentially speculative: they do not necessarily adapt to existing structures of supply and demand, but are based on expectations of how markets will or can develop or be developed. This introduces a source of endogenous change into the market mechanism itself: over and above changes in supply, demand and technology, there is an element of intrinsic uncertainty in the market which can be seen as the outcome of all entrepreneurs second-guessing what others, producers or consumers, will or might do. In this context the skills of 'reading' the market and 'feeling' the development of fashions and trends will become more important than finessing production methods. Another way of understanding this approach is to say that it is impossible to define 'given' needs and means, since no one knows exactly what products and tools are or can be used for. It is therefore inevitable that new uses and combinations will arise, by fruitful misunderstanding if not by deliberate search. The entrepreneur is the person who sets out to investigate these possibilities, if indeed they are not simply following their own private obsession.

The preceding position is largely intended to reflect the position of Hayek (see Hayek 1962, 1978). It is striking that while generally agreeing in the description of what actually occurs in competition and entrepreneurial activity, Kirzner makes the dynamics of the process appear to be completely the reverse, because he takes equilibrium rather than disequilibrium as his point of reference. He argues that entrepreneurial activity is equilibrating rather than disequilibrating. In order to do so he suggests that there are constant 'mistaken' choices which create the possibility for entrepreneurs to act as repairmen. For Kirzner, the fact that the economy is essentially a non-equilibrium process is the result of the constant reappearance of these 'mistaken' choices and decisions among individuals, based on the inevitable existence of a certain amount of ignorance about the actions and decisions of others (Kirzner 1973, pp. 11–17). Whereas Hayek's position sees the entrepreneur and entrepreneurial search as the creative power in the formation of markets, Kirzner's writing sometimes seems to make the entrepreneur into a fixer of the deficiencies of market information reminiscent of the pre-modern merchant.

Nevertheless, Hayek (who refers to an intimation of his approach in an article by Wieser) and Kirzner (who considers his own position to be based on that of Ludwig von Mises)[5] both agree that markets are 'churning' as a result of internal processes rather than simply reacting to external shifts in preferences and technology. They also both agree that individuals as economic actors and individuals as human beings whose aims and desires are constantly evolving cannot be rigorously separated, so there are no external data of preferences towards which market forces converge.

In contrast to these approaches the Schumpeterian model does not begin from any assumption of equilibrium in the sense usually understood in modern equilibrium theory but rather from a picture of economic life as a cyclical reproduction based on habit and custom. In a manner analogous to Marx, Schumpeter explains modernity as the irruption into this system of entrepreneurial activity as initially something interstitial. Entrepreneurship is seen as essentially innovative.

Schumpeter directs his whole argument towards explaining innovation and suggests that there are reasons why innovation does not take place uniformly but in waves. He further suggests that these waves of innovation can be correlated with and seen as the cause of at least some of the business cycles within capitalist systems. In the first instance this is because there are some innovations which immediately create an environment conducive to further innovations. There are 'leading' technologies which create a demand for new infrastructures of supplies, components, transportation, storage and maintenance. They also spill over into uses not initially envisaged. At first, the additional demand, financed by credit, which arises as entrepreneurs grasp the implications of new possibilities, energises the entire economy, even though some old technologies are made obsolete by the new ones, with attendant shrinkage and closures of old businesses. This is the 'boom' phase of the cycle. Eventually, though, there is a tendency for this expansionary phase to lose its impetus. This is seen as arising from the combination of several factors: the repayment of debt by those firms which have successfully ridden the boom wave coinciding with the collapse of older firms which have failed to adjust to the new situation. But while Schumpeter believes that some retrenchment would in any case be necessary and lead to cycles, he feels that the main reason why booms are generally followed by crashes is informational.

It could be supposed that the demand for goods previously generated by the older failing industries and the demand for capital previously generated by the new industries which are now becoming profitable and self-financing could be continued by the appearance of a new wave of innovation. Schumpeter believes that the main reason why this does not happen is that in the wake of the disruption caused by the first innovative wave no one is in a position to make rational calculations about the viability of further innovations. There must be a period of stabilisation before a new wave of innovation can begin. Schumpeter does not feel that the crash, although often heralded by a series of disastrous misinvestments, can be seen as the result of a lack of wisdom on the part of the initiators of such projects. While many projects which appeared rational during the boom may founder after the crash, this does not mean that these projects were over-optimistic or represented an over-extension of the boom technologies. Rather, it is the difficulty of rationally estimating the viability of genuinely new innovations which prevents entrepreneurs from initiating more radical innovations, and to some extent leads to over-investment in 'me-too' enterprises. The real reason for the depression is not foolish misinvestment but wise non-investment. It will be suggested here that this could usefully be interpreted as the exhaustion of the value of the entrepreneurial 'tacit know-ledge' acquired within the older market situation in the newly given situation. Creative destruction will disrupt the structures, perhaps the institutions, of markets, and therefore make 'entrepreneurial', 'managerial, 'capitalist' and even some 'innovative' skills and knowledge redundant at the same time as those of the more technical aspects of the older systems of production – marketing, transport, storage, repair and so on.

Schumpeter further proceeds to argue that innovation financed by credit is both the defining characteristic of capitalism as it has existed in Europe since medieval times, and the only source of all profit and non-usurious interest.[6] He sees all profits as quasi-rents on innovations, which the market process will begin to erode as soon as knowledge of the innovation is diffused. He regards interest as the price which entrepreneurs pay to divert purchasing power from existing undertakings into new ones. He considers that in a stationary economy there would be no innovations and thus no profits, and no demand for capital and thus no interest. Schumpeter does not believe that profit is the reward for either risk, which can be insured against, or waiting, as more productive methods involving waiting will completely replace less productive ones (Schumpeter 1961, pp. 32–3 and 36–8). Rather like Marx, he believes that all operating profits are redistributed shares of a common surplus, except that he believes that this surplus is generated by innovation and does not exist at all in a stationary society.

Schumpeter's notion of 'waves of creative destruction' is thus the result of a kind of quantum constraint on the interface of economics and technology, which arises because there are certain innovations which necessarily have a certain 'scale' attached to them. The pure equilibrium model sees the market as a process which adapts to external shocks but is intrinsically both static and stationary. The entrepreneurial search model sees an intrinsic source of disequilibrium within the economic process itself, and in some of Hayek's formulation suggests that the economy will not remain static even if it is close to stationary in real terms. Schumpeter's model sees technology as only one source of entrepreneurial innovation among others, but with the specific difference that some technologies are so basic that their introduction disrupts the process of economic calculation, which is only re-established after a period of stabilisation. This is why each of the major periods of boom and depression in the modern world economy can be correlated with the introduction and spread of a number of new technologies, particularly those of basic power provision, materials, transport and communications.

Schumpeter's model leads to the assumption that there will be considerable movement in the population of firms, since survival is dependent not merely on efficiency in day-to-day terms but on the rapidity with which firms respond to the possibilities offered by new technological and market trends. Entrepreneurial profits in Schumpeter's sense are likely to be reinvested in growth within the originating firm and lead to monopolies in the markets for the new products.

The skills which would be associated with the working of a Schumpeterian model in the boom period would be those of rapidly grasping the possibilities of new technologies, not as solutions to existing problems, but as the basis for completely new paradigms. The processes involved would be similar to those found on frontiers of science, in Polanyi's terms 'breaking out' and 'turning around', being able to use the results of present knowledge rapidly to hypothesise a new scheme of how things will work beyond the boundary of the presently known.

In summary, the simple Walrasian system suggests that the capitalist market economy is an embodiment of a principle which leads to equilibrium, but which must constantly adapt to external influences in the form of preference shifts and technologies. The Austrian systems suggest that the capitalist market economy is a system which produces within itself tendencies to disequilibrium. Kirzner's interpretation sees entrepreneurial activity as the major force leading to the establishment of equilibrium, which however is never achieved because the *homo agens* as opposed to the mere *homo economicus* does not separate the processes of preference formation from those of need satisfaction, so that the in-any-case necessarily imperfect information on which the majority of economic actors base their decisions must constantly be revised. Hayek's version regards entrepreneurial activity as the only way in which economic activity is co-ordinated, and therefore as establishing the universal system of prices and standards which is the basis of the idea of equilibrium, but he does not suppose that this process is an adaptation to any external given set of needs or preferences. By contrast with these approaches, Schumpeter sees two distinct mechanisms: the equilibrium nature of natural economies, which is largely a product of the power of habit and custom, within which there is evolution and adaptation but only on very long time scales; and the capitalist system, within which the entrepreneur and the capitalist in combination create a dynamic of innovation and of capital formation which only arises from the profits of innovation.

Can capitalism survive?

Schumpeter felt that the likely trend of the future would be that capitalism would give way to socialism. By this he did not mean Soviet-style state ownership and centralised planning, but the 'corporation' model of public ownership as implemented in the UK and more widely by social democratic parties. His major argument for this was that the 'institutionalisation' of innovation as a departmentalised activity of major corporations robbed private individual- istic capitalism of its major claim to existence – the opportunity for the 'little man' to achieve something. Without the constant renewal of the capitalist and entrepreneurial classes there would be little public support for the continua- tion of a privately owned corporate economy in comparison with a publicly controlled corporate economy. He did not follow the path of Hayek, who argued that even if all scientific truth were discovered once and for all, there would never be a shortage of suggestions for reorganising production in ways which would produce more profit than continuation of existing patterns. It may be that Schumpeter considered that the permutation of organisational innovations would not be sufficient to generate the ideological support necessary for the continuation of capitalism.

Since 1970 there has been an apparent reversal of this trend. A massive part of the growth of the world economy during these years has arisen from the entrance of many large nations into the developed world, following the paths of institutional evolution initially developed in the 'First', developed world. This could therefore be a transient phenomenon. Likewise, the collapse of many sectors of the economies of the advanced world due to labour-cost competition from developing countries will eventually cease as wage levels and other operating costs in the developing countries rise with fuller employment of labour and other inputs. The recognition that the advanced countries could not maintain their ossified structures in the face of these phenomena initially gave rise to Thatcherism and Reaganism, under the sway of which many markets were liberalised. However, despite extensive privatisation the proportion of GDP absorbed by the state has not significantly fallen; and despite measures to activate the small and medium business sector the role of the major corporations in the economy has not significantly altered. The factors seen by Schumpeter as sapping the political will to maintain private capitalism could therefore be expected to reappear when the adjustments made necessary by the extension of the capitalist model to the entire world are complete.

Schumpeter's views about the end of capitalism may be easily misunderstood by anyone who does not start from his starting point. Many liberal thinkers might see the end of capitalism as the end of personal freedom because they see economic life as the absolute basis of personal freedom. From this point of view, the market economy is individual freedom 'writ large' and its decline would be equivalent to the decline of the freedom of the individual. Schumpeter does believe in a universal, trans-historical role for the individual, but he does not see it as especially linked to economics. His theory of entrepreneurship posits a universal process of individuals seeking to introduce novelty into human affairs, and mobilising wider resources to achieve this. He applauds the creation of capitalism for two reasons: because it channels economic resources into technological innovations, which he regards as on balance enormously positive; but also because it channels entrepreneurial enterprise away from conquest and piracy. Modern capitalism leads to peace not only because peace promotes trade, but because the energies which previously went into war are diverted into the economy. He can envisage that entrepreneurship in politics, religion, science and art can absorb the energies which might be set free by the exhaustion of the innovative potential of the economy. In terms of the debate we have reviewed above, when radical scientific discovery and the trickle-down effects of this in economising the resource input into all possible economic activities are complete, it is not obvious that the purely market-oriented innovations envisaged by Kirzner or Hayek would draw as much of the innovative talent of society into the economy as presently occurs. However, Schumpeter, like many of his contemporaries, not only supposed this process to be nearer completion than it now appears to be but did not envisage the processes of the extension of market penetration into the economy which we are now witnessing.

We suggest that another factor not foreseen by Schumpeter may have emerged during recent decades, and may have more importance than any politically motivated liberalisation of markets. This is the reduction of transaction costs made possible by new information and communication technologies, which can have a series of effects centrally important to the relevance of Schumpeterian theories of entrepreneurship and innovation. Within the firm the greater ease of using internal pricing systems means that there can be more efficient comparison of the cost-effectiveness of internal and external sourcing. The market and price comparisons penetrate into the internal workings of the firm to a greater extent than was previously possible. These comparisons may lead to the outsourcing of many activities which were previously carried out within the firm. This may relate to service activities but also to basic production activities. Large-scale outsourcing creates new markets within which entrepreneurial activity can lead to innovations in the provision of services which were previously hidden from market forces. Every new wave of outsourcing can provide an opportunity for a new wave of entrepreneurial innovation. Services which were judged on the basis of adequacy within the organisation come to be judged in comparative terms of price and quality when they are available through an active market.

As markets proliferate, the importance of being client-centred or client-facing grows as the direct communication with final users of products and services becomes a source of information for new innovative possibilities. From being a backroom activity, speculatively carried out and then market-tested, innovation is increasingly directly market-driven. We will return to the question of the specificity of the skills and knowledges which develop in the market process in line with this model after reviewing the relevance of Michael Polanyi's theories to the prevailing model of competitive advantage.

Theories of capability, core competency and competitive advantage

Within business writing, 'tacit knowledge' has been related to the questions of firms' core competencies and comparative advantage. In this context we examine developments in the investigation of implicit learning and distributed cognition as characteristic features of teamwork.

The major premise of the debate about core competency and comparative advantage is that firms build up a stock of skills which is tailored to a specific field of activity and can only with effort and difficulty (and a significant possibility of failure) be transferred or even extended into other areas. It will be useful to consider this problem from the perspective of Boisot's threefold categorisation of tacit knowledge (as introduced above): that which can only be made explicit at a cost; that which is ineradicable, at least in the sense that it builds up again around any core of explicit knowledge; and that which is so taken for granted that it becomes apparent only against the contrast of a new environment. In each of these cases it will be seen that the problem is compounded when some part of the tacit element of skills and knowledge is distributed knowledge. In this case the knowledge is only embodied in action by a team, which means that it is difficult to separate the knowledge generated by the particular make-up and division of labour of the particular team from that which might be generic to different circumstances.

The arguments of Penrose (1995) and Porter (1998) suggest that 'tacit knowledge' as usually understood would be a large part of the package of 'core competency', because the knowledge involved in firms which pursue a course of development in new products and processes within a particular branch of a particular sector will include knowledge both about what they do well and how, and about what they have found to be the problems about attempting to expand into neighbouring areas and why it is not worthwhile. This knowledge of all the things that went wrong and were seen to be unworkable is the kind of knowledge which can be made explicit only at a non-trivial cost.[7] Of course, it is also the case that this type of knowledge may only be 'true' from a particular perspective on a fitness landscape – that is, that a new product or process may only be unattainable from where this particular firm is at present; but the point is that the firm is actually there now and cannot transplant itself directly into a different starting point from which the ascent to the new product or process would be easier. This applies even when there are written records of failed projects, whether scientific, technological or process-oriented – it is the personal knowledge which is embodied into the insight that a particular suggestion is in danger of setting off down a road to failure that is important, rather than the simple facts about previous failures.

Nelson and Winter (1982) provide the most extensive discussion known to us in the economic literature of Polanyi's concept of tacit knowledge.[8] This is in a context of the extended analogy drawn between the skills and routines of an individual and of an organisation, here a firm (developed over pp. 72–138, and see pp. 76–82 for the detailed examination of tacit knowledge). This includes a rare recognition of the necessary interrelatedness of 'psycho-motor skills' and active patterns of perception (pp. 76–8). The authors use the concept of tacit knowledge to argue against an exaggerated estimation of the role of choice in economic life, suggesting that tacit knowledge involves implicit perception of factors, which means that the scope of choice is often much less than would be suggested by consideration of the formally available possibilities, so that for the skilled person choice is often automatic or not a real factor at all (pp. 65–71 and 82–5).[9]

In the further development of their argument, the authors are not concerned with specifically entrepreneurial skills. They consider a model in which firms have developed routines between which they can switch resources, whereby one of the routines is precisely Schumpeter's 'routinised innovation' aiming at leading technologically, while another is R&D directed to imitation.[10] They proceed to investigate the advantages of various allocations of resources between these applications of R&D. Leading into this, in the chapter 'Routine as Organizational Memory' (pp. 99–107) the authors develop the claim that 'organizations *remember* by *doing*' in terms of how routines function not merely as rituals or rhythms but as signalling devices, and conversely how individuals develop the ability to interpret these signals as such and perform the appropriate actions. Although no longer explicitly referring to Polanyi, the situation described is one in which individuals have made the routine of the organisation into a probe or heuristic for their own actions, proceeding from formal instructions or from a variety of implicit inferences to interpret the signals generated by the progress of other parts of the wider process as indications of the need to follow one particular procedure rather than another in particular cases.

Nelson and Winter (1982, p. 76) introduce Polanyi with the words, 'On the simple observation, "We know more than we can tell", Polanyi built an entire philosophical system.' They begin their discussion of him in the context of a theory of the role of skills, and cite Polanyi's own statement: 'I shall take as my clue for this investigation the well-known fact that the aim of a skillful performance is achieved by the observance of a set of rules which are not known as such to the person following them' (from Polanyi 1958, p. 49). The authors explain that while an instructor may be confident of being able to articulate the knowledge necessary to exercise a skill, 'the detailed instruction offered typically consists of a list of subskills to be executed in sequence, and the instructions neither convey the ability to perform the subskills with the requisite efficiency nor assure the smooth integration of those subskills into the main skill' (Nelson and Winter 1982, p. 77). Rather, useful instruction consists of a combination of verbal instruction and demonstration, imitation and critique of the learner's attempts. Reactivating a rusty skill makes even more obvious the superiority of tacit knowledge over explicit knowledge (p. 78). However, good instructors do have the capacity to 'discover introspectively, and then articulate for the student, much of the knowledge that ordinarily remains tacit' (p. 78), but they do not rely on communicating this knowledge explicitly but integrate it into their programme of modelling the student's behaviour.

Nelson and Winter see the need to analyse 'the determinants of the degree of tacitness' (p. 80) in different (learning) situations. They specify:

1   Situations in which explicit information cannot be communicated within the time of the action aimed at, while pre- and post-trial communication cannot give a full impression of the simultaneity of the experiences of the action. (It seems the use of video could increase the value of pre- and post-trial analysis of the action.) Slowing down the action during tuition does not necessarily completely solve this problem as the subsequent speeding up of the action may not be a simple process. (In fact, the slow and fast actions may not be done in the same way at all.) They use the examples of tennis playing and typing.

2   Situations in which the explicit knowledge is of 'limited causal depth' (p. 81). Taking the example of swimming, the knowledge of how the body achieves buoyancy cannot be communicated to those parts of the body which actually perform the actions necessary to achieve this. Knowledge of the underlying process may give the beginner more confidence, but does not cause their ability to be efficacious.

3   Attempts to make tacit knowledge explicit knowledge can become incoherent through overemphasis on details which break up the unity of the message. The authors suggest (in line with Polanyi's own interests, although they may not have known this) that visual aids can reduce this problem. They conclude with a statement which remains relevant to any practice-oriented analysis of tacit knowledge:

> much operational knowledge remains tacit because it cannot be articulated fast enough, because it is impossible to articulate all that is necessary to a successful performance, and because language cannot simultaneously serve to describe relationships and characterize the things related. This observation provides us with at least a starting point for assessing the relative significance of tacit knowledge in different situations.
>
> (Nelson and Winter 1982, pp. 81–2)

In their next section Nelson and Winter discuss skills in terms of the prevailing economic paradigm of choice between the use of different methods and resources. They conclude that choice is mostly associated with inadequate knowledge, and that expertise leads practitioners to much more assured decisions which are often not experienced as choices at all because the answer is so obvious. Within this context, the role of tacit knowledge reappears when they state that

> The picture is further complicated by the fact that particular units of behavior, of whatever scale, are not assigned permanently and uniquely to the categories 'chosen' and 'automatic'. Rather, circumstances affecting the immediate goals and attention allocation of the performer are an important determinant of whether a particular unit [of behavior] is run off automatically, or as a result of deliberate choice . . . The picture is complex, but in general it seems to contrast sharply with emphasis that orthodoxy gives to choice in the explanation of behavior, and also with its insistence on a strict conceptual distinction between capability and choice . . . Skillful acts of selection from the available options are constituents of the main skill itself: they are 'choices' embedded in a capability.
>
> (Nelson and Winter 1982, pp. 83–4)

Nelson and Winter situate their use of the tacit knowledge concept within an analysis of the existing understanding of the problem of knowledge within economics. Crudely put, firms were seen as economic actors on the market, combining input factors in different proportions in order to produce products which could be sold on the market, while attempting to maximise their return by using inputs in the most economic way and producing a mix of outputs which would bring in the largest possible income. Information about products, processes and markets was seen as strictly dichotomised between publicly available information, which was regarded as free and equally accessible to all firms, and new information, which had to be created by research and development. R&D in turn was seen as a production process which produced information at predictable cost. Cost would therefore determine whether R&D would be carried out internally or purchased. The cost of processing information within the firm was regarded as negligible or as sunk in the overheads of management costs. Within this idealised view, knowledge is either on paper, whether drawn from public knowledge or from internal R&D, or embodied in workers who are available on the labour market and are supposed to embody a generic kind of professional or trade knowledge. If there is a shortage of such people, price rises will motivate more individuals to become trained.

Against a background such as this, Nelson and Winter begin to use the concept of 'bounded rationality', as developed by Herbert Simon.[11] They develop an argument (pp. 65–71) which dissolves economic orthodoxy's absolute separation between capability and choice. Firms are entities within which there are no strict boundaries between the supposed economic factor inputs and an abstract level of managerial or entrepreneurial choice. Decisions about what to do are made at the edge of existing capabilities and only rarely or never at the level of choosing which capabilities the firm should have. In the same way, decisions about production are never made on the basis of perfect knowledge of all markets, processes and products, and there is no way of knowing what is the optimal level of investment in finding out such things. Nelson and Winter's interest in tacit knowledge is thus framed by the assumptions that the precise limits of the firm's capabilities are not known and that the precise limits of the firm's knowledge of its own markets, products and processes are not known.

This background already creates an opening for the use of the concept of tacit knowledge as a boundary area separating the firm from perfect knowledge as idealised in economic theory. This would create scope for mapping tacit knowledge and modelling the potential advantage of making some of it explicit. Nelson and Winter have a more precise area of interest in tacit knowledge, however, as they are interested in developing an evolutionary theory of economics. They consider that any evolutionary theory must settle on some particular unit of evolution; and any such unit must be something which is capable of replication and variation. They accept the firm as their unit, and within the firm they designate the 'routine' as the DNA or genes of the firm, which provide simultaneously for replication and for variation.

This is explained in the following terms: routines are the capabilities which the firm possesses that enable it to do particular things in particular ways. The firm can generally replicate its own routines in response to increased demand much more rapidly than other firms can replicate them. This is what creates economic sectors and niches: the fact that routines are not easily replicable without constant reference to an already functioning routine. Competitors and new entrants can replicate routines by R&D, reverse engineering, industrial espionage or poaching staff, but such replication is never as easy for outsiders as for the firm which has working routines of its own. Within this context it can be seen that it is never clear exactly what replication means, since not all of the aspects of a routine will be captured by any explicit description. All mediation through explicit descriptions will result in some loss of detail, however fine the mesh is drawn, while imitation will always carry over some elements of unspoken and unreflected practice. We will return later to the corollary of this, which is that sub-optimal practices are also transmitted by the same processes of induction and imitation of existing practices.

However, within particular economic sectors, some firms will also excel in their capacity to build new capability through working up new routines. Competitive advantage will result from continuous experimentation giving rise to new routines from which successful variants can be selected for replication.

Thus, a firm which is large enough to experiment with variations in routines has the best of both worlds: both its old and its new routines are relatively protected against replication by outsiders, while both can be replicated within the organisation in proportion to demand for its products. The transfer of tacit knowledge within the firm is a necessary part of this process of replication. This is generally accepted by the entire subsequent management-oriented literature on tacit knowledge.

However, we have still not exhausted the insights of Nelson and Winter, since we must now revert to the lack of an ultimate distinction between capability and choice, or between skill and decision, at the level of the manager or entrepreneur. Schumpeter in his later work discussed the possibility of the 'routinisation' of innovation itself. R&D departments are generally seen as the embodiment of this routinised innovation. However, Schumpeter also defined innovation as the 'carrying out of new combinations' within the existing framework of markets and resource utilisation. There is therefore always an element of tacit knowledge of the environment of the firm involved in all decisions to adopt particular R&D strategies. Nelson and Winter see both R&D and innovation as further routines which the firm may embody, and conclude that 'the skills of the highly trained operations manager, scientist or manager are reflected in characteristic, highly patterned forms of problem-solving' (Nelson and Winter 1982, p. 136).

This discovery of tacit knowledge as a key factor in competitive advantage, and of the related question of the inextricable unity of capability and decision within routines, was developed in terms of the competitive market economy, but it has implications beyond this. The civil service, military, emergency services and non-governmental organisations and healthcare services also face the problem of replicating best practice, and may find that the circulation of explicit knowledge is insufficient to ensure genuine replication of routines. This will also apply to those areas within the market economy which ought to be outside the competitive process, such as health and safety, environmental issues, and staff payment and insurance procedures. Transfer of tacit knowledge in all of these areas is part of the process of successful replication of routines, which becomes more acute as the dissemination of information on new technologies, procedures and regulations is put online or distributed in CD form.

Tacit knowledge as the natural environment of incremental innovation

We now examine the relevance of tacit knowledge, first in the specific form developed by Michael Polanyi, then in the wider senses of the term used by organisation theorists, some of which are seen to be related to Granovetter's 'embeddedness'.

Polanyi's distinction between the subsidiary and focal modes of attention could be relevant to the skills of the entrepreneur in 'seeing' opportunities which are missed by others.[12] The ability to 'gestalt' wider situations without being locked onto the everyday or customary uses and meanings of things is not an innate gift but a result of familiarity with a wide range of both situations and transformations. The gift of seeing 'new combinations' (in Schumpeter's words) is a version of the ability to gestalt-switch between wholes and parts (although Schumpeter makes it clear that practical energy to bring about the new combinations is also necessary for the entrepreneur). The exercise of an ability to see that a firm or project is not working, and why not, can be easily understood in the context of Polanyi's understanding of the inseparable nature of perception and judgement. The dynamic of the tacit component of knowledge can be used to understand why some people are able to anticipate trends, not only in cultural products which may personally interest them, but in the most impersonal markets, such as those for basic staple commodities.

Following their distinctive interpretation, Nonaka and Takeuchi (1995, p. 60) took up Polanyi's distinction of tacit and explicit knowledge and attempted to make it more 'practical'. This might seem unfair if it suggests that Polanyi's own work remained unpractical: Polanyi used the most up-to-date psychological and neurological research in developing his concepts, but his interest in the practical use of tacit knowledge was largely expressed in terms of the tacit knowledge of scientists and doctors. Nonaka and Takeuchi are concerned with the organisational environment of knowledge in business, and with discovering procedures for creating new knowledge by unusual combinations of existing knowledge. They set up a grid of the possible interactions between tacit and explicit knowledge. The process from tacit to explicit knowledge is the standard procedure by which activities are formalised and codified for the benefit of persons who need to acquire the knowledge other than by direct induction; the converse process is the way in which we begin to internalise the schemata and procedures of such instructions when we begin to become familiar with the context, and the judgements and actions involved become second nature. They suggest that there is considerable potential in confronting the explicit knowledge held at different levels within the same organisation. In contrast with the 'Western' model, they suggest that the greatest single gain for the organisation can be from the sharing of tacit knowledge. This is not to be understood as 'multi-tasking', which facilitates the transfer of staff in response to demand shifts or emergencies, but as a basic procedure for making all participants aware of the real problems of other parts of the organisation. This is claimed to lead to the overcoming of many of the misunderstandings and failures of communication between the research, development, production and marketing wings of organisations, leading to greater market responsiveness. At the same time, they are aware that global organisations in an open labour market situation need a large degree of formalisation of tacit knowledge.

However, this entire discussion is pursued using an equivalence of tacit knowledge with stocks of existing knowledge, if not necessarily in the form of identifiable 'facts'. The authors often give the impression that tacit knowledge is essentially comprehensible as an internalised familiarity with a particular context which cannot be communicated to others because it is not formalised. Their discussion does not transmit the idea that tacit knowledge should be understood as an altered perception which is active in creating new knowledge because it is sensitised to particular kinds of evidence and interprets this evidence in accordance with particular patterns or schemas.

As previously reported, Boisot (1998, p. 57) develops a threefold model of tacit knowledge:

1   His first paradigm is knowledge which is 'taken for granted'. This is knowledge which is so ubiquitous within a particular context that there has never been any need to formalise it. It is only when one 'culture' (national, business) comes into contact with another which does not share this knowledge that there is a realisation that this knowledge exists and is not universal.
2   Boisot claims that his second paradigm is that of Polanyi, and characterises it as 'Things that are not said because nobody fully understands them. They remain elusive and inarticulate.' This seems to miss the dynamic aspect of Polanyi's idea, which is that although some existing tacit knowledge can always be formalised, the new formal knowledge will generate a new layer of tacit knowledge in its application. More fundamentally, it suffers the same deficiency as Nonaka and Takeuchi's understanding, by which it is probably influenced, when it focuses on 'things' being said or unsaid, rather than on the processes of generation of patterns in perception.
3   The third paradigm is that of knowledge which can be articulated, at least by some people, but only at a non-trivial cost. Boisot considers that this is the kind of knowledge investigated by Nonaka and Takeuchi.

Granovetter (1985) reminds us that in the 1930s, 1940s and 1950s a series of sociological investigations showed that there was a considerable degree of co-operation, trust, negotiation and sharing of knowledge both within and between organisations which was ignored by normative organisational theory but was often essential to meeting the targets of organisations and their component units. The knowledge involved in these contacts is in many cases tacit knowledge, both in the sense that it is the kind of knowledge which is largely acquired unconsciously, and in the sense that it is often not reported, not because it is illicit (though this may sometimes be the case), but because it is 'taken for granted'. Reading of more recent literature on governance[13] suggests that Polanyi's wider understanding of personal knowledge, as the development of a series of schemas which allow rapid, almost unconscious, perception of the implications of situations, will have an application to understanding the way in which people learn to process information differently in different governance contexts. Thus, in Boisot's terminology, markets, hierarchies, clans and fiefs – or, as in other literatures, industrial districts and networks – will give rise to different 'default' assumptions about the significance of particular facts and changes. The ability to envision 'new combinations' will be relative to such institutional-governance backgrounds.

Corporate R&D

The 'tacit knowledge' of the market which is the basis of the action of the entrepreneur in Schumpeter's first theory of creative destruction may be contrasted with the corporate R&D-led approach outlined in his second theory.

Schumpeter always considered the entrepreneurial function to be intrinsically distinct from that of the capitalist, the manager or the inventor. The entrepreneur is solely that person who conceives and develops new economic combinations. The capitalist is the person who stakes their own money on the success or failure of economic undertakings, whether new or established. The manager is the person who ensures that all the necessary processes are carried out on a day-to-day basis. The inventor is the person who originates a new process, product, material or technology. In many instances these functions may be carried out by a single person. The situation becomes interesting when the roles of entrepreneur and capitalist diverge. The capitalist stakes their money and expects to gain whatever profits are produced, less some negotiated payment to the entrepreneur. But the capitalist must have some criteria for choosing which entrepreneurs to support, or which of their projects to support, or a strategy or method for how to spread their investments between different entrepreneurs and projects. The capitalist or their advisers must therefore have or suppose that they have some access to a 'meta-entrepreneurial' knowledge which allows them to decide which entrepreneurial suggestions are plausible and viable. The crudest method is to support projects put forward by experienced and proven entrepreneurs.

In *Capitalism, Socialism and Democracy*, Schumpeter (1976) put forward the view that the entrepreneurial function could be routinised[14] – a proposal which is generally discussed in terms of the prevalence of 'corporate R&D' organised in large divisions within capitalist organisations. He also suggested that this could lead to a more regular flow of innovation, to some extent evening out the 'waves' of creative destruction. Fifty years later, during which we have experienced another boom apparently based on air travel, transistorisation and pharmaceuticals,[15] we must suppose ourselves on the brink of another wave based on digitisation, genetic engineering, micro-engineering and new materials. While these inventions have mostly been the result of massive corporate and government-led R&D, their application to business has often been led by small firms which are entrepreneurial in precisely Schumpeter's sense of combining knowledge of new technologies with a vision of how to use them in the current market context (often based on insight into com-municational, entertainment and other consumer uses for what had been envisaged as 'big' technologies).[16] The corporate R&D which is applied to the investigation of the market as such has by contrast been found to be most successful only within the established tracks of firm-specific capabilities and competencies, and even here success is far from secure (Pavitt 1994, pp. 357–8). It does not prevent new products and new markets growing up outside the control of the large organisations (evidenced most disastrously by IBM and the PC market). There is therefore still a role for the skills of the 'non-corporate' entrepreneur.

The tacit knowledge of entrepreneurs

Different theories of the working of competition lead to different estimates of the importance and value of different kinds of tacit knowledge for entrepreneurs.

One of the answers to the problematic of whether firms are truly profit-maximising was that intentions were less important than outcomes; only those firms whose behaviour approximated to that expected on the basis of profit maximisation would survive, so it did not matter by what reasoning or other processes decisions were arrived at. (This can be equated with the investigation of behaviour in the biological sciences: long-term investigation of animal behaviour, whether in controlled experiments or in observation of natural behaviour, suggests that choices approximate to optimal pay-offs under circumstances where the individual animals are not assumed to be operating conscious utility rankings and preference curves.) However, this means that a significant number of individuals must be making decisions which in fact lead to the survival of their organisations under the given circumstances. These decisions may not lead to maximising of any parameter, but may nevertheless keep the firm competitive. It may be assumed that many of these decisions are the result of the internalisation of knowledge acquired by implicit learning. The individuals learn to do what their colleagues do, within a tolerable margin. Clearly this kind of routine will be less viable in times of general confusion than in times of general stability. Conversely, deviating from this pattern will have costs which only strong personal inclination or the clear perception of large potential gains will justify.

Schumpeter saw the skills of the entrepreneur primarily as in having the ability and energy to gestalt and practically implement 'new combinations', a phrase which contains by implication the idea that the elements of these new combinations must first be extracted from their previous embeddedness in 'old combinations'.[17] He does not see 'being an entrepreneur' as necessarily a lifetime activity; on the contrary, he often implies that most successful entrepreneurs will eventually settle down as 'managers' of their growing businesses.[18] In order to be able to go beyond merely envisioning a new possibility and to proceed actively to set up new combinations, it is generally necessary to have an overview of the availability of inputs. Schumpeter's theory assumes that entrepreneurs are more likely to emerge in large numbers during the depression phase of a cycle precisely because of the existence of unused or underused resources. The entrepreneur is favoured at this time by the relative ease of imagining other more productive uses of these resources. As the boom proceeds, with some new technologies experiencing increasing returns and many subsidiary activities riding in their train providing new infrastructural services and goods, there comes a point when it is no longer easy to see how resources could be put to better use. Even if new technologies or products are developed, it is not necessarily easy to see how they can be profitable, because the context of their possible use is made uncertain by continuing changes in other related areas. This is the context of the 'informational' side of Schumpeter's explanation of the crash which often leads into the depression.[19]

Waves of creative destruction and stocks of tacit knowledge

We return to the question of the effects of creative destruction and other forms of market-led or technology-led innovation on stocks of tacit knowledge and other knowledge assets.[20] It is clear that the introduction of the predominant new technologies of the 'machinery', 'railway', 'electrical' and 'automobile' revolutions led to a massive destruction of infrastructures, skills and thereby tacit and implicit knowledge. This was associated with a constant reduction in the application and value of 'rural' as opposed to 'urban' skills and knowledge. This has led to a massive reduction in the familiarity of most modern individuals with a wide range of materials, tools and processes.[21] The last thirty years has seen a steady move from 'production' occupations into 'service' and office occupations, in terms of real activities, although this effect has been exaggerated by the 'outsourcing' of many service activities from industrial organisations. In the past, infrastructures have been out of step with new technologies and become a drag on innovation.[22] At present, many major Western economies may be said to be running ahead of real technological changes: while there is a genuine shortage of some special skills, the educational system as a whole is apparently geared to speculatively producing a highly skilled and highly educated workforce against the assumption that this will be necessary in the competitive 'world of tomorrow'. It may be that this emphasis on formal education is actually eating away at real levels of tacit knowledge which the considerations above suggest are best acquired through learning-by-doing. On the other hand, early familiarity with the world of cyberspace may be necessary not in order simply to manipulate and work in this environment, but above all to be able to see the entrepreneurial possibilities within this new paradigm. It is the ability to gestalt-switch between parts and wholes which will facilitate the envisioning of 'new combinations'.

Having built up the background to our argument, we now put forward some speculative suggestions about the relationship of personal knowledge and tacit knowing, entrepreneurial skills, and creative destruction. The personal knowledge which is specific to the entrepreneur will consist in the first instance of knowledge about networks of contacts, about the working of markets, about the actual and potential uses of technologies and systems of work organisation, and about the existence of unused or underutilised resources. Added to this there must be a heuristic or gestalt-switching ability to imagine elements of various existing systems in new combinations in the service of a new leading idea. There must also be the ability to organise individuals and organisations to bring about this scheme, and ability to persuade potential investors of the viability of the project, unless the entrepreneur has funds of their own. The existence of explicit or codified sources of information can never substitute for the existence of individuals who embody and can work with implicit forms of the 'same' knowledge and skill. Only practice can facilitate the necessary degree of tacit inference and gestalt switching which is necessary to produce and adjust new combinations rapidly as a real skill rather than simply as a formal exercise.

There are obviously large areas of overlap between tacit knowing and the heuristics of tacit inference which are used in everyday business operations and management and those specific to the entrepreneurial function. The valorisation of these knowledge resources in 'everyday' use is subject to the general problems of the valorisation of skills: on the one hand, the difficulty of capturing the real cost of creating them; on the other, the limitations or 'granularity' of their transferability to other uses, in-house or with other firms.

In the Schumpeterian scheme, entrepreneurial activity may be exercised within a division of labour. The central entrepreneurial vision may be carried out by instructions to a number of collaborators through formal directives, or elements of the 'envisioning' process itself may be delegated to collaborators who then autonomously produce their own sub-programmes for carrying out the tasks within the wider vision. The 'learning organisation' based on the Japanese model is an example of the attempt to spread the entrepreneurial function to the entire workforce. However, there are limitations on this process. First, we must remember that for Schumpeter the entrepreneur is not merely the possessor of a vision, but must also have the energy and independence to struggle to make it a reality. There is obviously a degree to which the remuneration of managers reflects a potential conflict between the manager's actual value as a manager and their potential value if they used their skills and knowledge as an entrepreneur. There is also the problem of exceeding 'requisite variety'; that is to say that entrepreneurial activities within the firm could become too disparate. These factors together may explain the attraction of the American model of relatively easy exit and re-entry from management to independent or spin-off entrepreneurship.

Within the Schumpeterian scheme it is only innovation which produces genuine growth and profit. The creation of entrepreneurial skills is therefore the key to economic growth. However, creative destruction as understood by Schumpeter must have the effect of cyclically destroying the value of much of the tacit knowledge on which these skills are based. The disruption of market channels and of infrastructures of supply, storage, maintenance, repair, training and expertise which follows from the obsolescence of older 'leading technologies' makes rational planning of new ventures more difficult. The tipping which makes the further use of old technologies impossible cuts off some avenues of sourcing. It is difficult to decide whether to commit investment in areas without standards and dominant technologies. The destruction of the relevance of stocks of 'entrepreneurial' tacit knowledge and of the patterns of tacit inference based on them can be seen as playing a role in the Schumpeterian explanation for the failure of booms to continue or to shade more gradually into a following depression.

In recent years we have seen governments of the advanced economies emphasising the need for their populations to acquire the new skills necessary for the 'New Economy', stressing the need for a wider circle of active entrepreneurs who would take advantage of the opportunities it will generate. These formal skills are the tip of an iceberg compared to the tacit knowledge of markets, technologies and organisational procedures which enable some individuals to become effective entrepreneurs. The profile of skills which will really be taken up by the processes of the New Economy, including the relevant component of tacit knowledge, will remain problematic as long as the contours of the infrastructures and standards of the New Economy have not crystallised. The generic skills which have been seen as useful for the 'information society' may be rapidly outdated by the appearance of effective biotechnology and nanotechnology. Just as it has become accepted that the employed workforce will need several phases of retraining in their lifetime, it may be that entrepreneurial knowledge and skill will also have to adjust to several upheavals. Whereas genuine 'entrepreneurs' might well move on from declining markets to growth markets within those economies which succeed in keeping up, 'entrepreneurs' who have been primed by the state to participate in me-too enterprises will easily be left behind by radically new market dynamics.

Collaborative innovation between competitors with different core competencies

The 'routinisation' of R&D was at one time seen as a possible source of continual growth. The period since the end of the Second World War has seen such a process on one level, in that there has been a continuous process of miniaturisation and the reduction of the costs of all inputs through automation and robotic tools, lighter, stronger materials, and lower power requirements. However, much of this advance has become so predictable that it is discounted in advance, and serves only to create small advantages of one player over others within established markets for a limited period. The type of entrepreneurial tacit knowledge which has been created by this form of development was that of the possibilities of incremental innovation along more or less clear lines of development. The decline of IBM and Apple when they, in different ways, failed to predict the shape of the new PC market may be seen as a failure of over-routinisation, while the way in which they both subsequently managed to re-emerge in a different form may be seen as a return to genuine entrepreneurial innovation, creating new markets for new products: IBM as a 'solutions' provider; Apple as a content-media manager.

Baumol (1993) provides the major theoretical insight into a new understanding of the role of innovation under the circumstances of the extension of the market. As each organisation is forced to concentrate on its core competency and to shed service activities and other operations which can be provided by the market, there is an increase in the potential for collaborative innovation between groups of firms with complementary core competencies. As compared to the paradigm of a race to achieve a decisive breakthrough, he considers that 'much more common . . . is the case in which the innovations of competing firms and firms in different countries are not only different, but complementary' (Baumol 1993, p. 171). Even when firms compete in the same markets, producing similar ranges of goods, they can still benefit by sharing innovations if their innovative strength is in different areas, and if, as is usually the case, it would be prohibitively expensive for each of them to try to achieve the same degree of expertise in all areas. Furthermore, the sharing of technology and innovation can increase the size of the market for any single producer as diffusion of the fundamental technology will produce greater take-up due to the spread of complementary products. The increasing complexity of the market and the growth of offers of complementary products will make it easier for each firm to concentrate on and develop further its main competitive advantage and core business. In this way Baumol's views feed into Stiglitz's insight that development should not simply be seen as linear growth but above all as growth of complexity and of markets and institutions.[23] The availability of inputs and complementary goods allows innovators to take full advantage of their innovations, and as each firm is thus allowed to develop its core business and competitive advantage, this in turn makes collaboration between them more advantageous.

A similar point is made from a quite different starting point by Richard Nelson (1996). Asking 'Why Do Firms Differ?', he begins by asking why monopoly is a bad thing, and, instead of settling for the monopoly price explanation, argues that monopoly will fail to produce the levels of innovation which competition can, because monopoly is 'unlikely to generate the variety of new routines, and the attendant shifts in resource allocation, on which economic progress depends' (Nelson 1996, p. 119). Even without deliberate experimentation and innovation, a number of firms will produce differences in the way in which they do things on which the pressures of evolution can work. The more intense competition is, the more firms will be forced to experiment both with the way they do things and in whether they should be doing some things at all. In some sense, all firms attempt to escape from the pressures of market competition, but if they cannot achieve monopoly, they can achieve excellence in some aspect of their business which will enable them to collaborate with others with complementary excellences. The market and competition not only play an evolutionary role by selecting between alternatives but produce the complexity which leads to the appearance of a variety of alternatives to be selected.

The thrust of this argument is continued by Nelson in his essay 'Capitalism as an Engine of Progress' (Nelson 1996, pp. 52–83). Drawing on a collaborative survey of industry understandings of innovation (Levin *et al.* 1987), he reports that in most industries patents and secrecy are less important in gaining the benefits from innovation than the first-mover advantage, and that this is so because 'Producing complex systems involves many components and many details that need to be got right; much of this learning proceeds on-line rather than in the lab' (p. 64: in 1990, when this essay was first published in the journal *Research Policy*, 'on-line' still meant on the *production* line). Nelson then claims, 'In these industries, firms tend to develop differentiated areas of special competence' (p. 64), a finding which agrees with those of Baumol. This situation would seem to call for attention to the competencies involved in 'getting things right', both because these could otherwise be lost, and because the maintenance of differentiated areas of competency requires continual improvement of these competencies. It might also require sharing some of the information with partner firms that have complementary competencies in order to converge technologies which they are incorporating into a joint product.

By contrast, 'First-mover advantages and patent protection were rated less effective in protecting process innovation than in product innovation in almost all industries' (Nelson 1996, p. 65). However, this did not result in a preference for using secrecy as a means of protecting process advantages; rather, it led to a disinclination to invest in developing process advantages at all, so that 'the bulk of industrial R&D is directed towards new or improved products' (p. 65). The result of this was that 'In many industries, the bulk of [process innovation] work is done by upstream firms, material and equipment suppliers' (p. 66). Drawing on work along similar lines by Eric von Hippel (1988), Nelson (1996, p. 66) concludes that:

> the locus of inventive activity is determined, in part at least, by where the ability to appropriate returns is greatest. When an industry is fragmented, if a process innovation is made by a firm in that industry, its level of use is likely to be quite limited given the relative insensitivity of market share to process innovation. But if process innovations come in the form of new materials and equipment produced by upstream firms, the market is the industry as a whole. It should be noted here that the incentives that locate process innovations upstream reflect real efficiency gains to the economy as a whole.

In a later development of the research of von Hippel and Urban, Henkel and von Hippel (2003) drew the conclusion that there was great scope for co-operation and knowledge transfer between equipment producers and lead users, particularly those lead users who were experiencing problems with products and who were themselves experimenting with adapting or improvising changes to existing products. They found that:

> user innovators often have sticky, need-related information that manufacturers lack. On the other hand manufacturers typically know more about how to turn a prototype into a robust product, and how to manufacture it at low cost . . . innovative activity by users can embody sticky user need information in a form that can be easily transferred to manufacturers, enabling manufacturers to become more successful in new product development. Second, user and manufacturer knowledge concerning innovations are to some degree complementary. This implies that users and manufacturers can benefit from each other's innovations rather than compete with each other. This in turn implies a welfare-enhancing [partial] internalization of spill-overs.
>
> (Henkel and von Hippel 2003, p. 8)

In their investigation of innovation in twentieth-century America, Mowery and Rosenberg (1998, pp. 175–6) report that in the years before 1940, the US pattern of innovation was based not on a strong national programme of scientific research, but rather on the engineering capability to absorb the results of European science and to turn these into products for a mass market. Although they do not put it this way, American success in this period was similar to that of post-First World War Japan. But despite the USA having become the leading power in basic science research by dint of its political priorities and its overwhelming economic superiority, the authors consider that the underlying picture in innovation has not really changed, as science has not contributed to post-war innovation as much as development:

> most of what is referred to as 'R&D' is something other than science. Roughly two-thirds of US R&D investment constitutes 'D', which is to say that most R&D expenditures are devoted to product design and testing, redesign, improvements in manufacturing processes, and so forth. Most R&D has not been science, whether basic or applied.
>
> (Mowery and Rosenberg 1998, p. 173)

This supports the assumption that incremental improvement in product and process design is crucial to national as well as firm-competitive advantage.

We have identified three different scenarios in which the diffusion or sharing of new technology is already seen as an essential element in innovation, several of which are likely to become more important rather than less:

- the replication of newly developed routines within innovating firms;
- the exchange of innovations and the convergence of innovations between partners in research and development projects;

- the diffusion 'downstream' of the methods of use of new equipment and materials developed within particular industries and for which producers will want to encourage maximum take-up by ensuring that clients are able to use the innovations optimally.

We would argue that the mapping of the tacit component of skills, knowledge and routines (in Nelson and Winter's sense) will play an increasingly important role in the effective and efficient diffusion of new technologies and materials. We would also suggest that the framework for such a mapping will in many cases be provided by the embedding of qualitative and quantitative measurements of the implicit and tacit elements of skills within existing systems of competency management and personal development. But first we will examine a further factor in the equation, which follows on from the point made by Nelson regarding the innovation failures of monopoly. The next chapter will examine the exposure of an increasing number of routines to competitive pressures due to the substantial reduction in transaction costs made possible by new ICTs.

6 Tacit knowledge in the New Economy

Knowledge as the only surplus-producing factor – post-capitalist society

In 1993 the business analyst Peter Drucker argued that the traditional economic categories of land, capital and labour were being overtaken by knowledge as the source of profit.[1] What he meant by this was that in the global economy, where there is no market which is safe from new entrants who can reproduce the advantages of existing firms in terms of economic inputs, only knowledge remains as a competitive advantage which cannot easily be replicated. In Schumpeter's terms, if all profit is a quasi-rent on innovation, which will ultimately be eaten away by 'normal' competition, only a continuous process of innovation based on extending and developing existing sources of competitive advantage will protect firms from the pressures of the market. In the context of our investigation, the bodies of knowledge Drucker discusses will necessarily rest on a specific and dynamic mass of tacit and implicit components.

Explicit codified knowledge can only be protected by patents and copyright, which run out after a period of time, or by secrecy, which can work for recipes such as those for special blends of absinthe, but which is not advisable for more basic technologies which can be reinvented. Tacit knowledge cannot be replicated as easily as codified knowledge, because it is contextual. Nevertheless, tacit knowledge can be quite closely replicated by industrial espionage, reverse engineering or poaching staff. A potentiation of tacit knowledge is the tacit knowledge embodied in processes of continuous incremental innovation. The next step in potentiation is tacit knowledge which is not merely part of a process of continuous incremental improvement of products or processes, but which evolves in direct contact with the evolution of the demands and requirements of users. Firms attempt to produce knowledge about the preferences of consumers by direct questionnaires or by making projection from mass data. This in turn can be nuanced by maintaining personalised data together with some demographic facts about the individuals concerned, which allows the trends in individual consumption to be combined with population trends to map future demand more precisely. The most developed kind of market knowledge would be to ask consumers not merely what they want from what is on offer, but what they would like in the future.

Thus, there is a value chain and a knowledge chain. The commanding position on the value chain, in relation to which all other positions on the chain are reduced to producing at the lowest margins, is that position which can access the information about market trends and which has the capacity to develop the new processes and products that will be required. Producers who fail to capture this kind of data may be upstaged by retailers who can interpose themselves between producers and their markets by being more responsive to new market trends (e.g. Amazon). Conversely, producers with tacit knowledge in one market and product can invade a neighbouring market because they have the ability to develop a new product using their existing systems (e.g. Apple/iPod). Firms can abandon any fixed product and make themselves into solution providers, using their wide knowledge of how to develop products and processes (e.g. IBM). Across these examples knowledge is the key factor, but tacit knowledge and explicit knowledge play different roles in different economic sectors. An example at one extreme is the market for heavy earth-moving equipment, where the requirements of the product are reasonably fixed, but the technology of the product and of the manufacturing process are subject to continual incremental improvement, requiring tacit knowledge of basic engineering processes and their relevance in development projects. At the opposite extreme is the apparel market, where knowledge of consumer behaviour, markets, fashions and innovative business models is essential.

For Drucker, the background to the sole value-creating role of knowledge, as with Schumpeter, is the mechanism of competition, which reduces all sources of 'rent' on other inputs to the production process. The combination of the approaches of Drucker and Schumpeter leads to the outcome that the only source of profit is the innovative use of knowledge. This is disguised by the imperfection of existing markets, but there are currently processes under way which bring reality closer to the model of perfect competition. One of these is the abolition of legal and political obstacles to the free movement of capital, goods and services, including labour, but it could be argued that these political changes are themselves driven by the acceptance of the inevitability of more fundamental reasons.[2] Foremost among these is the despatialisation of markets allowed by the development of new information and communication technologies, which can be encapsulated in the concept of the creation of a cyberspace. The implications of this will be now be explored.

The global market – abolition of space

Real space is not of course abolished by anything. Reduction of transport costs has been a continuous process for several hundred years, and reduction of the time taken to fly persons or cargoes around the world has been stable for nearly forty years. What is referred to as the abolition of space is the fact that space is no longer a serious factor in the production and marketing of 'despatialised' goods and services. Software, intellectual and entertainment content, information and advice, banking, insurance and administration can all in principle be sourced from anywhere. As societies become more affluent, these goods and services, some of which are 'intangible', make up an increasing part of the economy.

Political obstacles and infrastructural weakness prevent some nations from fully participating in this process at the present time. On the other hand, lack of legal and regulatory frameworks allows some nations to participate fully in the black market for illicitly reproduced software and entertainment content. In this context it should be mentioned that *this* despatialisation has nothing intrin-sically to do with the relocation of industrial and assembly work from the advanced nations to the developing nations. While it is the case that both are at present driven by wage-rate differentials, their long-term prognosis is different, since global equalisation of wage rates and tax regimes would stop the migration of manufacture, and lead to the re-emergence of various local competitive advantages based on natural resources. The despatialisation of intellectual content is by contrast intrinsic and irreversible.

The extension of the market is driven by another aspect of the reduction of costs of communication and storage of data, and particularly by the inter-connectedness of financial databases. This is the reduction of transaction costs and includes the reduction of the cost of all financial transactions as they no longer rely on the circulation of coins and notes, requiring the maintenance of the security of these, or on the processing of cheques, a labour-intensive activity. In economic doctrine the term 'transaction cost' has acquired the wider meaning of all of the open and hidden costs of undertaking a transaction on the market. This will be explained in greater detail later, but here it suffices to say that cyberspace, the Internet and the World Wide Web produce potential reductions in all forms of transaction costs. The result of this is potentially an enormous extension of the role of the market in every area of life.

Transaction costs and the boundaries of markets and sectors

The transaction cost theory of the firm states that it is transaction costs in the widest sense which explain why firms ever do more than one core activity (Coase 1988). If it were not for transaction costs there would still be economies of scale within any particular field of production, and joint product processes in some industries, but there would be no reason for vertical integration, or for firms to organise their own research, accountancy, cleaning, transport, etc. The market would in principle mediate between every single physically or con-ceptually discrete process of production. If market competition can be supposed to produce greater efficiency, then such a situation would increase social wealth, and would do so to the direct benefit of each firm. Transaction costs, including the need to insure or self-insure against market uncertainty, are what make it more rational to carry out within the firm activities which in principle might be carried out more efficiently by a dedicated producer of those particular goods or services. The loss of efficiency which follows from the fact that many activities are carried on within closed environments in which there is no effective comparison with the efficiency of other producers is paid for by the reduction of transaction costs.[3]

It follows that any substantial reduction in the cost of transaction accounting or market research would tend to encourage companies to shed non-core activities and use more external suppliers, which *ceteris paribus* would increase total social wealth. Thus, information technology is implicated in a process which not only will reduce social costs and increase social wealth proportionately, but, by opening up areas of production to market competition that were previously sheltered within the environment of the firm, will make possible a process of further efficiency discoveries. So, alongside privatisation and deregulation, reduction of transaction costs by electronic information processing will produce a substantial extension of the market. The concomitant emergence of specialist providers of outsourced products creates competitive pressure towards innovation in these activities which is lacking while they remain fragmented within myriad organisations where they are peripheral to the survival of the firm.

This is particularly relevant in markets which have historically been highly integrated. Arora *et al.* (1996) discuss the transaction cost approach to the outcome of market situations where a number of vertically integrated companies compete in a sector market. Each of the companies is unlikely to be producing all of the integrated products as efficiently as possible, but their deficiencies may be compensating so that no one company is able to out-compete the others. Most or all of the companies could be beaten in competition by a specialised producer of most or all of the integrated products, but because all the firms are integrated there is no market for the intermediate products, or the market is not big enough to justify production at a level which would initially be competitive. This situation may have arisen because initially, when the market was first created by the development of a new kind of product, there was no established market for the intermediate products, so that transaction cost analysis indicates that integration would have had to be superior to market searching. But this situation then becomes self-reproducing since the integrated companies prevent producers of intermediate products from ever achieving a market share at which they would out-compete the integrated firms. Even when the integrated state of the market is due to some other historical cause, or where there are substantial savings in transaction costs in integration, a dynamic approach would see that the obscuring of each individual stage of production within the integrated firms removes them from the full effect of the entrepreneurial discovery process and is likely to delay innovation. Thus the model of Arora *et al.* identifies scenarios in which transaction cost reductions which led to deintegration would give rise to a dynamic process of improvement of efficiency in each stage of the previously integrated production processes.

An analogous model to that of Arora *et al.* is discussed by Langlois (1995) as arising when a new technology ('systemic' innovation) is discovered which in order to achieve viability must create its own network of supply and distribution: he cites the example of frozen meat.[4] Although the slaughtering, processing, freezing, shipping and distribution of frozen meat are activities which might well be more efficiently carried out by independent firms, they initially had to be organised by the freezers, because neither slaughterers nor distributors were convinced of the value of the new technology, and the technology for shipping had to be developed in tandem with that for freezing itself. A similar case could be made for the aggressive and now often regretted promotion of the internal combustion engine at the expense of railways and electric tramlines. Although in the final situation deintegration might produce greater efficiency, initially the promoters of the core technologies concerned were forced to create integrated industries because no market for complementary or intermediate products existed. This situation may persist after it has ceased to be necessary, but may be unfrozen by radical changes in levels of transaction costs and thus of entry costs. Langlois (2001, pp. 88–9) has since discussed the benefits of technology spillover which arise in 'network effects' when consumers converge on particular technology standards so that the skills connected with them become generalised while the familiarity of consumers with the possible alternatives makes modular production of a wide range of models within the paradigm economic since the basic principles are generic.

Even where there are massive economies of scale in the centralised handling of information for large organisations, better information technology enables these economies to be still further increased by the transfer of such activities to external agencies which specialise in these particular forms of information processing. Increasingly, firms will realise that economies of scale in internal provision of non-core services have in the past blinded them to the possibility that specialised firms operating in a competitive market are more likely to innovate and produce genuine increases in efficiency compared to traditional methods of service provision. The reality of this is currently sometimes obscured by the simultaneous but fortuitous use of less regulated labour.

Conversely, the penetration of the market mechanism into the structure of large firms, whether through deintegration or 'virtualisation', is likely to remove many of the obstacles which have prevented the participation of SMEs in some sector markets,[5] as long as SMEs themselves can develop the specialisations which will allow them to find a niche in the deintegrated production structures. This in turn will depend on the use of new technologies to facilitate the exchange of information which would allow SMEs to meet the technical and scheduling requirements of customers.[6]

It may however be the case that the extension of the market mechanism will have the effect of increasing the frictional rate of unemployment. In the 1950s and 1960s it was thought that a realistic rate of frictional unemployment was between 2 and 3 per cent, but this was in a context of high transaction costs of employment. One effect of such costs is the hoarding of labour which is underutilised in normal times as an insurance against sudden high demand. If employees are regarded as 'suppliers' of labour, then the logic of market extension leads firms to look for their labour supplies externally: that is to say, on the open market rather than by internal 'stockpiling', in this case by hoarding labour. The more 'flexible' labour market eventually leads to the erosion of the 'full-time job' as workers become suppliers of 'flexible' amounts of labour time in an open market. This process can be further facilitated by the grading of labour, which further reduces transaction costs. The costs of education and training can be regarded as legitimately part of the 'costs' of the 'supplier' of labour when the 'worker' is in this way abolished and replaced by a market partner. A rate of resource unemployment of 5 or 6 per cent, which may be a reasonable frictional rate under the new conditions, will actually be smeared over 10 to 15 per cent of the population whose 'offer' of labour is not fully taken up.

The same extension of market mechanisms facilitated by reduction of transaction costs could explain the growth of differential payment of labour. In the 1950s and 1960s, employers attempted to introduce payment schemes based on productivity. These measured gross output of components weighted by some considerations of wastage and quality. The problem with this was that it was impossible to measure the contribution of any particular production process to the profitability of the final product. Thus, while management could attempt to standardise and de-skill individual processes in order to reduce the ostensible market value of the labour input, they had no way of genuinely calculating the value of the worker's output to the firm. So long as all production took place within the firm, every stage of the process was a bottleneck and its value in principle infinite. This was realised by trade unions, both in the sense that they were aware that for the firm the entire production process was a unified whole which could be interrupted at any point, which was the basis of the unions' power, and in the sense that they intuited that payment based purely on skill and speed left out some aspects of the 'value' of the process to the firm. A more market-open firm is able to make direct comparisons of the value of internal production processes, or stages thereof, with external competitors. Reduction of transaction costs also makes possible the 'virtual' splitting of firms into cost centres. Together these processes make it possible to reward labour in line with the real contribution of profit centres and work teams to the firm, and reduce the need to de-skill and regiment labour.[7] The corollary of this is the widening of differentials among the labour force.

There are analogous ways of showing that the reduction of transaction costs, largely through new technologies of information processing, is capable not only of approximating more closely a 'perfect' market, but of allowing a more thorough commoditisation of all kinds of hitherto 'anomalous' inputs, such as intellectual property, land, credit, finite resources and unique objects.

The next step will be to extend the approach to pollution and sustainable ecologies.[8]

There is an element of international competition in the area of the market-opening potential of information technologies. The major market-oriented economies must each consider the use of information technology not only to achieve a one-off reduction of transaction costs, but to utilise the potential of this for creating a wave of efficiency gains through the possibilities for increasing the penetration of the market.

What are transaction costs?

The transaction costs of a firm are the costs which arise from participation in a market together with insurance against the additional risks that a firm incurs by doing so. The alternative to entering a market is self-provision. Ultimately the firm must enter some market somewhere to obtain some initial inputs over and above the labour power of the entrepreneur themself. The question is one of determining the limits of the activity of the firm within a particular market situation, which will be characterised by local historical factors producing a specific configuration of markets and firms. Having set themself the aim of producing a particular final good, the entrepreneur must decide how much of the manufacturing and finishing process, how much of the research and development, how much of the marketing and distribution, how much of the administration and cleaning will be done within the organisation by partners, management and employees, and how much will be externally supplied through the market. Transaction cost versus administration cost will also be relevant to the decision to centralise supply of materials and consumables within the organisation, in addition to considerations of cost reduction by bulk purchase and auditing. New technologies of communication, of transport and of information storage will always have simultaneous effects on transaction costs and administration costs, so the same new technology may lead to opposed effects in terms of firm expansion or shrinkage (or fragmentation) in different sectors or under different environmental conditions.[9]

Reductions in transaction costs are presumably a major factor in the clustering of firms, despite the adverse effects which clustering has on the rent and labour costs of the individual firms. The costs of finding price information, checking quality and ensuring contract compliance are all reduced by physical proximity. Except where production processes are inherently small enough for a small firm to produce directly for the final consumer from raw materials, small firms can be expected to cluster in cities and towns, and even in particular quarters, in order to reduce transaction costs. Within these clusters production processes will be fragmented, with different stages of the process being carried out by different firms. Large firms whose processes require location away from such clusters will tend to accumulate functions within the firm. Firms using patents or licences will be prepared to use more external suppliers, whereas the potential loss of confidentiality of a newly discovered or traditionally secret procedure will be a disincentive to the use of the market since information is given as well as acquired.

As opposed to training, which can be regarded as a stage in the production process and so is susceptible to standard transaction/administration cost analysis, the basic remuneration of employees is always a market transaction; the firm has no 'internal' source of labour (since the abolition of chattel slavery). Nevertheless, transaction cost analysis can be made relevant to two dilemmas faced by firms: first, whether to purchase labour in bulk and then to internally administer this resource without direct reference to market conditions; and second, whether to employ workers to work under the direction of the firm as opposed to switching to a market relationship which treats the worker as a contract partner in control of their own work processes.

An obstacle to attaining reduced transaction costs through new information and communications technologies (ICTs) is the initial investment in hardware and training. While these costs will inevitably fall with generalisation of the technology, in the short run they provide the basis for the formation of agencies and consultancies dedicated to making a profit by providing these services while passing on a large part of the cost savings to their clientele. The driving forces in the development of procedures to reduce transaction costs with these technologies are those organisations and firms which need to process millions of transactions each day, such as telephone companies, banks, stock exchanges, computer companies and booking agencies.

The perfect market is unattainable, but momentous shifts in approximating the perfect market can be achieved by taking advantage of developments in transport, communication and storage. The world market was created by railways and steamships and has been further deepened by air travel, cable, wireless and refrigeration. Recent developments in ICTs, principally satellite communications, fibre-optic cables, and the computing power and software necessary for the creation of the Internet, create possibilities for a significant extension of the market. Whereas the technologies mentioned have principally widened the market geographically, recent developments promise to facilitate a deepening of the market through the fragmentation of the firm.

According to the transaction cost theory of R.H. Coase (1988; originally devised in 1937), as developed by O.E. Williamson (1996), the firm has been constituted by the trade-off between transaction costs and administration costs. That is to say, that for the production of a given final product, the firm faces the choice between generating inputs internally or finding them on the market. Internal generation is associated with administration costs, labour management, bureaucracy, record-keeping and quality control, while external supply is associated with transaction costs, finding prices, checking specifications, communicating requirements, drawing up contracts, making payments, etc. The trade-off between administration and transaction costs will be different in different industries and within different environments, and will generate a nationally and regionally variable structure of small and large firms. The cheapening of communication channels affects both administrative costs and transaction costs, and the introduction of new technologies can have opposite effects in different industries, so that, for instance, the invention of the telephone could lead to growth of the firm in some industries, due to the disproportionate value of increases in efficiency of internal communication and co-ordination, and to the shedding of non-core activities in other industries, due to the easier access to the market as a source of supply of inputs.

As was the case with the telephone, new ICTs can have opposite effects in different industries, being used to extend the market in some and to expand the firm in others. But those economies will benefit more where on balance the effect is to extend the market and increase the scope for entrepreneurial inventiveness in increasing efficiency further. This in turn suggests that those economies benefiting most from ICTs will be those which develop standards most quickly, not just because they will benefit sooner from the absolute efficiency savings of lower ICT costs, but because this will contribute to the discovery of further efficiency savings through the extension of the market and the application of entrepreneurial discovery procedures to sub-processes which in other economies are hidden within the administered realm of the firm.

Transaction costs of labour

It is not obvious what transaction costs mean in regard to the labour market. Ultimately all labour is purchased on the market; none is produced inside the firm. One obvious transaction cost of labour is the advertisement of posts and the cost of processing applications and holding interviews. An 'internal labour market' means a preference for promotion and upgrading within the firm and possibly also a preference for recruitment by personal recommendation, but all supply still originates outside the firm. The costs incurred in such an 'internal' process could be regarded as administration costs relative to the trans-action costs of open recruitment. Another distinction could be made between hiring and firing as necessary and employing a fixed team of workers whose potential is not always fully utilised. Here the costs of hiring and firing could be regarded as more truly transactional costs, in contrast to the overhead costs of maintaining a team, which could be regarded as more analogous to administration costs. Perhaps it would be more appropriate to speak of 'market-near' transaction costs and 'market-distant' transaction costs for this distinction. Also relevant for an evaluation of the effects of new ICTs on transaction costs would be a distinction between the transaction costs of permanent, casual, agency and freelance labour. All processes which allow the assignment of a real market-price labour cost to the execution of a particular stage of the production process can be contrasted with those which constrain the apportionment of an arbitrary part of the price of a bundle of labour services to each cost-head or profit centre. Any change in transaction costs which allowed a more accurate assignment of real-price cost share would open the firm to the operation of the market mechanism and thus putatively provide information to improve efficiency.

International competition to set standards

Commodity trading between firms, final sales to consumers, and provision of financial services are all areas which will increasingly be conducted by electronic media. Those nations which set or rapidly accommodate to international standards in these media will have a competitive advantage in price and market position. A further competitive advantage may accrue to those states which take full advantage of the possibilities of the new media to encourage competition within their own markets, leading to efficiency gains which can give their firms an advantage over others. One area in which new media are essential to facilitate competition is in the deregulation and privatisation of utilities and transport. The fragmentation of provision of these services can only be combined with consumer satisfaction where a network of electronic media co-ordinates the interface between the different firms involved. Instances are the co-ordination of different rail firms (co-ordination between track providers and service providers, and co-ordination between service providers to present the consumer with a smooth transition from one provider to another), intercommunication between different telephone firms, and the shared use of basic water and power infrastructures by different firms. There would also be advantages to those states whose clearing houses can speed up banking procedures, or which might eventually be able to use direct electronic communication to abolish the need for clearing houses.

It has been suggested that the best preparation for international competition is stiff competition on the home market. This has been seen as a significant factor in Japanese and Korean success on the world market, and the need to increase competition as a spur to innovation has been seen as a motivation for the creation and widening of the single European market. The reduction of the cost of participating in a market should have the effect of widening the extent of that market, and should thus give rise to further efficiency gains through the encouragement of competition, with the further effect of increasing the fitness of participating firms for international competition.

Regional preconditions for new structures of the firm

The market will never be perfect, and one area in which this will become apparent is in the unwillingness of firms to trust their input supplies completely to the open market, depending entirely on price information. Information about reliability and quality will always be grounds for maintaining special relationships with proven suppliers, although this does not preclude some experimentation on the open market simultaneously. Therefore, an economy which successfully uses ICTs to extend the market and increase the number of firms will also have to make provision to network these firms. Firms developing new products will want to use ICTs to involve trusted partner firms without jeopardising their advantages.

Dual effect of new technologies

Reduced costs associated with storing, transmitting and processing information will not have a uniform effect of reducing transaction costs more, or more rapidly, than organisational costs. Different sectors of the economy will respond to cost changes in different ways, and the outcome will not necessarily be predictable, since assessment of transaction costs is often speculative and intuitive. For firms in industries which currently have an organisation orientation there may be no way of estimating the real costs of switching to a market orientation since there are no existing markets on which to discover prices. The reduction in inter-firm transaction costs which would lead to market penetration may be countered by reduced organisation costs either arising from the use of internal networking or because access to external databases in turn allows greater efficiency in internal operations. In some areas access to external databases may allow firms to dispense with the services of external consultants and agencies, reducing the market interaction of the firm overall. In some branches vertical integration may be encouraged by falling transaction costs in relations with the final consumer.

The alternatives of integration versus deintegration may be increasingly obviated in the areas of consumer goods, where new technologies allow producer firms to market directly to the final consumers. The combination of television advertising and credit card payment through voice telephone had already created a vast new market place for the direct sale of household and personal goods, which has been further extended by the Internet. Against this, however, the initial consumer resistance to the use of credit and debit cards on the Internet has led to the creation of a number of protected portals and market places within which consumers feel safer. This gives the firms in question access to enormous amounts of data about consumer behaviour, which underlines the value of the client-interface position at the end of the value/supply chain.

Both partners in any transaction have transaction costs. Firms which can decrease the transaction costs of their customers may gain a competitive advantage, whatever the effect on their own transaction and production costs. This reduction in transaction costs for the consumer need not be in the form of a financial saving, but may be a saving of time or a gain in convenience. The purchase of goods direct from manufacturers or from discount warehouses may be associated with a significant charge for postage or courier services, but if such purchasing is more convenient, the producer can benefit even while passing on to the consumer a large part of the wholesaler, retailer or inventory costs saved.

In some areas of technology social expectations run ahead of development of practical applications, being driven by science fiction or journalistic speculation on the potential for innovation. In some instances these expectations can be disappointed for decades or even centuries (see Elsner *et al.* 1994).

Entrepreneurs

Reaganite and Thatcherite political discourse presented the public with a populist and one-sidedly consumerist view of the value of the market as a source of consumer choice and market price mechanism-led efficiency. Absent from this discourse has been emphasis on the active role of the entrepreneur in creating the choices from which the consumer chooses and in creating new products and services ahead of expressed demand. While stress has been laid on the aspects of personal liberty in consumption, and on the role of competition as a corrective to bureaucratic waste and mediocrity, the more dynamic aspects of a market society have been underplayed. The Austrian conception (Hayek 1948 and 1978; Kirzner 1973 and 1992) of the role of the entrepreneur is based on the assumption that there is no real point of equilibrium in the economy, since all decisions are based on assumptions about the future activities and preferences of others which can only ever be approximations. In this area there can never be perfect knowledge since much of the knowledge which the model of the perfect market would presume to be in the public domain is in fact incommunicable and inexpressible. Thus, alongside those who create profits by seeing a gap in the market, inventing a new, more efficient productive process, or inventing a completely new product or technology, there will also be those who intuit a change in demand or preference and act on this intuition before the rest of the market. This role of the entrepreneur becomes more important as technological innovation accelerates, since every innovation alters the market environment of every other firm and makes possible new innovations in organisation and combinations of services. The labour market is affected by the acceleration of these processes as it becomes increasingly difficult to predict the precise mix of skills which the economy will require in the medium term.

We have separated our discussion of the effect of transaction costs from our section on more general innovation because the special effects which it can have, in terms of making use of market mechanisms, has the specific effect of increasing the penetration of competition to produce effects on processes which were previously hidden within the firm. But we do not intend to argue that transaction cost economics is a different realm from that of Schumpeterian economics. Rather, the effect of new ICTs on transaction costs is one of the effects of creative destruction, in this case the destruction of paper record-keeping and commercial transaction-logging by electronic technologies, together with the wider ease of accessing information on markets through electronic media.

The labour market as a search process

The labour market is an institution through which employers (buyers) select the services of employees (sellers). Manipulation of labour turnover can also help firms use the labour market as a hedge against the need to shed labour or reduce real wages. For employees, the labour market offers the possibility of pursuing a career structure through changes of employer, and gives access to possibilities of geographical relocation or career/skill changes. In recent decades, thought about the labour market has been dominated by the search for solutions to social problems thought to be caused by the failures of the labour market mechanism, long-term unemployment in certain localities, among older men and youth, and among the unskilled. This way of conceptualising the labour market as a source of these problems is misguided, since it overlooks the fact that these phenomena are the result of historic failures to innovate and upgrade capital and infrastructure, and would have eventually had these effects irrespective of whether labour allocation is effected through the market. The waves of redundancies experienced in the 1970s and 1980s and the doubling of the rate of 'natural' unemployment should rather be seen as the necessary preconditions for the labour market to fulfil its main function in the economy, as a medium for the price-led transfer of labour from less efficient firms to more efficient ones. The acknowledged rise in real incomes among skilled workers during the same period is a consequence of the fact that the labour market has been a success in freeing labour from less productive forms of employment. The collapse in the demand for less skilled labour during the same period is not itself the result of shifts in the balance of power between the partners in the labour market, but of extraneous factors. The political drive to deregulate the labour market, while partly ideologically motivated, was necessary because collective bargaining prevented the labour market from fulfilling its role as a market, since the best packages of wages and conditions (including security) were offered not by those firms which used labour most productively but by those historically linked to strong trade unions.

The 'Marshallian districts' discussed by Robertson and Langlois (1995; and see Marshall 1920) can be seen in this light as regions which are characterised not only by market competition between small, specialised producers but as clusters of employers within which there will be rapid mobility of labour between firms reflecting their (both employers' and employees') relative efficiency, facilitated by the low transaction costs of finding new workers for employers and of relocating to new employment sites for employees. This will have the added effect of transferring knowledge between firms with a tendency to pool useful knowledge in the firms most likely to make good use of it. This contrasts with the Japanese model, in which although there are much higher levels of sharing of knowledge and the secondment of staff between linked firms than in other models, there is much less movement of labour between competing firms or blocs of firms. Complaints about the lack of technology sharing in

UK firms have perhaps had a management-oriented bias, and have failed fully to grasp the degree of knowledge transfer which was a necessary concomitant of labour mobility within, for example, the Lancashire cotton, Yorkshire wool or Midlands engineering industries. It is an open question whether the new kind of post-Thatcher labour mobility is of this kind, since although it presumably facilitates the transfer of the most highly skilled and motivated workers into the most efficient firms, many workers presumably leave industries for new ones with a loss of the relevance of many of their skills.

Outsourcing and skills

Bhagwati (1997) has put forward an argument concerning the international effects of the processes whereby services splinter off from goods, or goods splinter off from services. He starts from the fact that where the provision of services is splintered away from the production of goods, this is generally because, for either technical or entrepreneurial reasons, the provision of services by outsourcing is more efficient than internal provision. Even where the initial splintering is for entrepreneurial rather than technical reasons, the process is subsequently more likely to be subjected to technological innovation than if it had remained subsumed within the parent industry. Conversely, where goods splinter off from services, it is the production of the goods which undergoes rapid technological development, while the service aspect is generally an intractable rump which is not amenable to technical change.

This distinction is amplified by the effects of disembodiment; that is to say, the possibility of using ICTs to reduce the need for spatial contact between the providers and users of services. Services which are splintered off from goods are likely to include a high proportion of activities which can be further rationalised by ICTs and which can therefore be located at increasing distances from the users. Services which are 'left behind' by the splintering away of goods are likely to be of the kind which cannot be separated spatially from the user.

Therefore, when discussing the relative 'growth' and 'shrinkage' of the 'goods' and 'services' sectors, it would be useful to distinguish processes by which goods emerge from services, or by which services emerge from goods, from each other and from the development of genuinely 'new' goods and services. This would provide indications of whether the goods or services in question would be likely to be technologically progressive, and also of whether they would be likely to be amenable to 'virtual' delivery systems and thus to relocation in sites with cheaper labour or rental costs. Conversely, the splintering of goods from services may lead to centralisation of production relative to the prior spread of provision of services. In either case there is a possibility of regional or international relocation. These questions all have obvious implications for the development and location of skills.

The knowledge worker and the flexible labour market

The flexible labour market is a genuine increase of the domain of the market; that is, it results from the ending of the hoarding and internal assignment of labour by large organisations which instead meet their labour requirements by calling on the market. This may at present mean calling on the unemployed, casually employed and part-time workers, but the existence of such labour unemployment is probably the result of medium-term processes such as low-wage Third World competition, capital restructuring and the skills obsolescence of older workers. The flexible labour market is unlikely to disappear when these factors recede in importance, since other factors, including transaction cost evolution, make the accessing of freelance and part-time labour directly or through agencies much easier, while the leaner firm will probably never be able to return to hoarding labour. Within this constellation the knowledge worker is in a special position, since firms must adjust to accelerating changes in their environment which only a dedicated specialist can keep up with, but most smaller firms cannot employ dedicated specialists in all relevant areas. The knowledge worker who is not positioned in a large corporation is thus forced to become a consultant working as a stand-alone business or in a small partnership. The proliferation of such persons will make necessary the provision of new forms of credit and insurance for such workers, and will lead to seeing the professional upgrading of such workers as an overhead of their business rather than as a form of training of personnel. The Internet will be increasingly necessary for such workers to keep up with new developments in their field.

The New Economy

Manuel Castells has put forward the most highly developed conceptualisation of the New Economy.[10] He sees the New Economy as characterised by the appearance of a new kind of economic meta-entity, the network enterprise, which is characterised by the networked communication between shifting groups of partners in development projects and in the ongoing production, marketing and improvement of products. The constitution of these partnerships is shifting from project to project, depending on their specific requirements, so that it is the pool of partners which engage in these ongoing collaborations that constitutes the network enterprise. In this sense the network enterprise is a disembodied version of the cluster or the industrial district. Because of the variety of inputs contributing to the development of products, the client-facing partner is the holder of the brand which guarantees the quality of the inputs to the final user. Castells sees the extension of the network communication through to the client (in wholesale and business-to-business) or the consumers (in retail) as essential to the feedback of forward information into the network. Another essential element is the possibility of sourcing inputs firm-internally, locally (cluster-internally) or globally. This is not as easy as it sounds when it is a question of high-tech components and skills being fed into an open-ended development project. Castells identifies a key element in the growth of global networks to be the creation in the developing nations of Asia of start-up, spin-off and buy-out firms by persons who have previously worked for multinationals or in global centres such as Silicon Valley. In a process analogous to the dismantling of the major Japanese firms some decades ago, networks are created based on information sharing and high levels of supervision of quality of inputs into the collaborative process. Castells considers that this process of clustering was also already under way in other economies decades ago, and that it was not initially caused by the Internet – some networks were experimenting with their own information-sharing technologies before the appearance of the Internet – but that the Internet has enabled the process to become global.

The 24/7 market is driven by the fact that the major stock, commodity and currency markets open and close in an overlapping way so that there is, in effect, a twenty-four-hour global market in stock, commodity and currency deals. Many major banks and multinational enterprises have subsidiaries which are listed on various stock exchanges, and they borrow, lend, underwrite and hedge on all markets. This means that the market estimation of the stock value of any major enterprise immediately has implications in all markets around the world, and that, conversely, interest rates all over the world have immediately notice-able effects on the profitability and hence on the stock price of most major corporations. This factor must be added to that of the altered status of the stock price, which no longer functions principally as an indicator of expected returns on capital over time, but as an indicator of the expected future value of the firm as an innovator, and of its ability to win or open new markets on the basis of new products and processes. At the same time, from the firm's own point of view, stock value is an index of its ability to raise new capital to finance these innovations. Castells sees the ability of firms to raise capital to pursue new innovations, and when necessary to buy other firms which either own new technology or provide access to new markets, as essential to the rapid execution of innovative insights. The switch from seeing shares primarily as sources of dividend income to being sources of rapid appreciation is a reflection of the changed dynamics of innovation away from the regular development of new products towards the creation and opening of new markets. A contributory factor to the ease of creating new markets is the Internet, which allows the launch of new products, business processes and product mixes that can rapidly gain large market share. If innovation is seen as involving the creation of new structures and therefore also as destructive of old structures, decisions to invest in one innovative enterprise rather than another can have real effects on the dynamics of the economy.

Contextual knowledge as the prime surplus-producing factor

The reason for this exploration of some aspects of the despatialised cyber-economy has been to underline what kinds of knowledge are necessary to begin to be innovative within this context. There are enormous potential gains in each stage of the opening up of the global despatialised market which is facilitated by the emergence of cyberspace. Castells (2001, p. 57) has emphasised that:

> While financial investors try to make money predicting future market behaviour, or simply betting on it, Internet entrepreneurs sell the future because they believe they can make it happen. They rely on their tech-nological know-how to create products and processes that they are convinced will conquer the market. Then the critical point is first to convince the financial markets that the future is there, then to try to sell the technology to the user – by all means – making the prediction work.

This statement perhaps requires some qualification. In Schumpeter's under-standing, all entrepreneurs have always tried to persuade investors to buy part of the future 'because they can make it happen'. There have also always been phases in which such investment has been drawn from the wider public rather than from the 'normal' share-owning public and institutions. The difference in the market for Internet shares has perhaps been that both institutions and other share buyers have been prepared to 'bet' on several different competing schemes to create a new future simultaneously. This is very interesting for our topic, since it indicates that there is a real uncertainty about what precise forms the 'future' will take. The failure of many dot.com companies does not in any way detract from the reality of the opportunities which existed and which may still exist, and which are shown by the phenomenal share value of those surviving cyberspace enterprises which have created a stable user base and market share.

7   Tacit knowledge, cyberspace and new imaging techniques

In this chapter we will open the question of whether the new medium of digitised information storage, transmission and broadcasting which we can designate as cyberspace, currently mediated by the hardware of the Internet and the software of the World Wide Web, will constitute or already constitutes a media revolution equivalent to the advent of printing and mass literacy. If so, this would have enormous implications for the understanding of how, in terms of Polanyi's concepts of commitment and indwelling, probes and heuristics, new patterns of accessing and absorbing data affect our ability tacitly to integrate these elements into a coherent gestalt. We cannot escape the fact that media studies were in effect initiated by Marshall McLuhan's claim that the advent of television was itself a media revolution comparable to the invention of writing or the spread of mass literacy due to printing. We must therefore make some effort to investigate the implications of the question of whether the cyberspace development is a continuation or a new beginning relative to the television era.

We began this book by explaining that we had found that in order to penetrate into the core of Polanyi's thought we had found it necessary to refer to his immediate sources and influences: Helmholtz, Dilthey, the gestalt movement and even contemporary positivism. This seemed to us a more fruitful approach than to rush to compare his work with that of contemporary thinkers who might be working to some extent in the same direction, but from very different presuppositions. We have presented the theories of Schumpeterian and evolutionary economics and innovation theory as a possible field of relevance and practical application for the concept of the tacit component of all skills and knowledge, without suggesting that there is any intrinsic connection between these theories and Polanyi's own body of concepts. In general we have not referred to the large body of business and organisation theory literature apparently treating tacit knowledge, since we have found that in most cases there is a tendency to try to situate tacit knowledge alongside other forms of knowledge, which is incompatible with what we take to be Polanyi's understanding of the tacit roots of all knowledge and skill.

If in this chapter we are diverging from this abstention to open up the possibility of a more direct interaction of Polanyi's ideas with those of the theory of media, it is because Polanyi himself drew much of his inspiration from investigation of the processes of interpretation of data through various contrived media. In particular he referred to the interpretation of X-rays, of crystallographic stereoscopies, of spectroscopy and of pathology slides. He was also interested in the use of charts, diagrams and animated films to illustrate economic and social trends and metabolisms. This seems to suggest that there is a basis for using his approach to contribute to the question of how we can learn to integrate or gestalt the information which we obtain through the channels of cyberspace. It also suggests that we could work towards an empirical investigation of the relevance of Polanyi's approach to the skills of using and interpreting the latest forms of scanners and imaging techniques. We therefore now present our understanding of the recent development of media theory.

When McLuhan published *The Gutenberg Galaxy* in 1962, his bibliography of around two hundred titles contained fewer than ten works which could be said to be thematically about the question he discusses, the uses and implications of media.[1] In the following decades several important works appeared which gave support to the idea that the transitions from orality to literacy with the invention of the alphabet and from elite to mass literacy through printing were linked with major changes in the psychological structure of knowledge, principally in the sense that epic poems were correlated with an encyclopedic approach to knowledge, elite literacy with a discursive approach, and mass literacy with the axiomatic-logical approach which claims to derive from mathematics and geometry.[2]

However, a counter-tendency has arisen which suggests that printing was not such a revolutionary divide as had been suggested, and that the formats and uses of books which we associate with printing had arisen before the technology itself. In fact the principles of the technology were known earlier, and Gutenberg was one of a circle of book producers who were struggling to perfect the technology precisely because there was a clear demand for the product. It was the development of a technology of producing paper which was suitable for printing which unleashed the print revolution rather than the idea of printing itself. It would also be possible to see television as the realisation of a demand which had previously given rise to the cinema, and to re-envisage the Internet and cyberspace as equivalent responses to a need rather than as technologies which appear from nowhere and suddenly revolutionise sensibilities. Nevertheless, we must consider the possibility that information technologies do have an effect on the ways in which we process information, and that the digital media may therefore have an effect on patterns of the tacit component of our information-processing skills.

One contrast which plays a prominent part in much of the literature is that of linearity as against the synoptic or side-by-side presentation of information. The striking characteristic of modern books, such as novels and other fiction, is that the text proceeds from beginning to end in a single stream without distraction of any other text on the page. The prevalence of this format has spread to 'popular' non-fiction works of all kinds, reflecting an aversion of the 'average' reader to visual complexity on the page. The encyclopedia has remained the last bastion of a style which was once prevalent in many non-fiction works, in which there are not merely footnotes, but marginal notes, marginal headings and additional passages of information which bite into the main text, sometimes not even enclosed in a box but marked out only by a different font. One information-processing explanation of this is that the average rapid reader does not absorb the text word-by-word, but subconsciously scans the entire line and perhaps the one or two following lines below, priming themself for what is to follow. This habit of reading would be disrupted by the presence of extraneous text which does not constitute part of the stream of text being followed.

The contrast to this is the format on which the Internet, television and many commercial market information systems are converging, which is both synoptic and dynamic. The synoptic aspect consists of the combination of different elements, using text, tables, real images, icons and diagrams in juxtaposition. The dynamic element can be applied to any or all of these, with text in ticker-tape form, video and live streamed images, animated icons, and tables and diagrams which are regularly updated with new price or other statistical input. The formats of television, the Internet and commercial in-house systems are now rapidly converging, a process driven by the transfer from analogue to digital television transmission and the resulting convergence of the underlying technology. Before making too much of this evolution, we should remember that newspapers always retained a more synoptic format, disambiguated by the use of frames, and that newspapers specialising in the presentation of financial or gambling information have more complicated formats than general-circulation papers. The revolutionary aspect of the new format is therefore rather to be seen in its dynamic aspect.

This brings us back to the claims made by Marshall McLuhan that television itself brought about a revolution in information-processing sensibilities which was concretised by the 'generation gap'. This phrase refers to the interpretation of the beginnings of consumer culture in the 1960s as a fundamental loss of common values between generations caused by the redundancy of the cultural forms by which those values had previously been transmitted. These claims can be relativised in a number of ways: they ignore the effect of prosperity and full employment in the advanced nations in the 1960s; they ignore the fact that the generation of the 1950s was itself seen as anomalous by many sociologists; and they ignore the underground psychological effects of the two world wars. Despite this, the claim that television had profound effects on sensibilities and information-processing faculties, perhaps precisely on those who were previously only weakly integrated into literate culture, cannot be ignored.

Probes and heuristics in the digitised market place

Ubiquity

Polanyi sees probes and heuristics as extensions of the self. The person who is attuned to using a tool as a probe has established a pattern of contact with parts of reality outside the limits of the body other than those provided by sight, hearing and smell. The combined effects of the three senses of touch, proprio-sensitivity and balance allow us to interpret events at a distance as directly as those at our fingertips. Heuristics extend the patterns of expectations and reliance on expectations from physical things to patterns of events and causation. Neither probes nor heuristics essentially depend on language or literacy. There are heuristics of the interpretation of climate, vegetation, animal and human behaviour which reside on the boundary of conscious and unconscious thought, implicit and explicit learning. Nevertheless, in modern urban societies many heuristics have arisen which depend on and integrate the powers of literacy, print and information systems, such as those of markets, transportation systems and commercial sport. In the last 150 years these systems have integrated the use of communication systems such as the telegraph, radio and television, and the heuristics involved have evolved to take for granted and rely on the information provided by these media. At this stage in their evolution, many of these heuristics still relied on physical presence at a place which was specially equipped with all of the technology to absorb and simultaneously display the information from these various sources. Stock, commodity, currency and insurance market trends, the current state of transport systems, and the progress and outcome of sport were all things which could be completely transparent only at informational hubs where all available data was displayed and updated. A second rank of information was provided by specialist newspapers which provided daily updates on market and sporting information, supplemented by a reduced selection of information in the evening newspapers.

The first effect of cyberspace, as mediated by the Internet and the World Wide Web, was that the information previously available only within these informational hubs is in principle available anywhere, in step with the availability of the same data to all other users of the system. Some data is freely available, some only by subscription, but this is consonant with the inherited business structure of many markets themselves, which are open only to members who pay for the facilities provided.

The availability of data as a stream can have different effects in two directions, standardising and diversifying, producing convergent and divergent trends in the forms of heuristics in use by practitioners. Among wider circles of users, the prevalent commercially available formats of data presentation will have a standardising and converging effect, as new circles of users who were previously dependent on paper sources of information are able to take advantage of streamed data. Some specialist organisations will however choose to produce their own forms of presentation of the raw data, producing new channels of analysis and recombination of the data. Investment organisations have taken advantage of this to develop expert systems which produce buying and selling recommendations, and some have even automated the use of this, but this does not concern us here except in so far as the output of such systems constitutes an additional source of input among others for human decision-makers. The dynamics of change mean that human experts will continue to have a role, even if this role involves taking continuous cognisance of the recommendations of expert systems. This is because the virtue of expert systems, over and above speed of calculation, consists in not being unduly influenced by the bias of the most recent input. In organisations which need to operate in markets or other contexts which are subject to contextual change, reliance on expert systems can never be total. The expert system becomes one among other sources of input into expert decisions.

The decisions of experts within the traditional market places and control centres were formed by the experience of data which was presented in the same form for everyone, on various forms of listings and mappings. Different individuals had different patterns of behaviour, and different degrees of taking advantage of the possibilities of human contact with other actors in the process, who were usually within the same building at the relevant times. Different personal preferences and patterns of experience meant that the heuristics of individuals evolved in different ways. The fixed frame of this was nevertheless the standardised format of the presentation and distribution of the institutionally given data. The possibilities of reformatting and selecting from this data mean that the possibilities of divergence of individual heuristics are now wider and can take more fixed forms. This has the immediate effect that behaviour may diverge more widely. However, it also means that there can be experimentation with the formation of heuristics by deliberately varying one's exposure to different sources and combinations of data. This can allow the emergence of new patterns, which may have been obscured by other forms of presentation of the data. In terms of expertise, good patterns are those which constrain the significance of phenomena, so that meaning emerges more clearly.[3] This approach presents the possibility of developing information delivery systems which facilitate certain forms of decision-making and choice. In Polanyi's terms we can facilitate the emergence of physiognomies, configurations which are recognisable as favourable or unfavourable combinations of symptoms, with a corresponding activation of the schemata of which responses are the most relevant.

Despatialisation

Cyberspace does not abolish or even transcend real space, but it does mean that in many regards distance is no longer a significant factor in cost. If you do your business through the channels of cyberspace, then the operating costs of using cyberspace are roughly equivalent everywhere. The economic effects of this are primarily seen in terms of the migration of business to places where the other costs – labour, premises, taxation – are lowest, and because there are great global differences in these costs, there is currently a relocation of those businesses, or of those services within businesses, which can take advantage of these disparities. This has been discussed earlier in relation to the phenomenon of ICT-facilitated transaction cost reductions. But this aspect of despatialisation, which one might call the passive aspect, will eventually become less important than what could be called the active aspect of despatialisation. The integration of mobile telephony with the media formats of the Internet means that portals into cyberspace are now themselves essentially ubiquitous.

If the portals of input into cyberspace can be located anywhere, and if they can be mobile, and if individuals and organisations adapt themselves to work exclusively with ICT-mediated input, this means that the effective reach of the senses is global. This brings us back to McLuhan's analysis of the fundamental power of television, of making the world present to us in our living room. However, television is essentially a passive phenomenon, even though we can now choose from hundreds of channels and alter the screen display parameters. This is perhaps a large part of why it is seen by McLuhan as so overwhelming, since we can only choose to enter into it or escape from it. If we have interaction, however limited, with an environment at the other end of a cyberspace connection, then we can begin to develop specific heuristics which give that particular environment meaning for us and make it into one of *our* spaces. The processes of commitment and indwelling can begin to extend our space of assumptions and expectations into this extended space.

Active despatialisation means that we can interact with any space with which we can establish interactive contact, and that we can exercise our integrative powers to make sense of the environment with which we interact through this channel. The most extreme versions of this at present are tele-surgery and other forms of distance use of investigative systems and repair tools. Once tools are developed which mediate electronically between the input from human hands (or even from other human-generated signals, such as eye movement) and the interventions of a machine-powered tool, the delaying effect of distance between the human and the tool, although in extreme cases not insignificant, allows direct response to ongoing events in a way which allows the human being to feel that they are 'there'. In this sense the abolition of space means that we ourselves are 'ubiquitous' wherever we have an ongoing power of direct intervention with immediate feedback. We will then also develop a set of assumptions and expectations about the way in which this particular environment works and therefore also a capacity to react to otherwise mundane experience events in that environment as shocking and unexpected.

Virtuality

Virtual reality was initially developed as a way of playing with unreal worlds, an extension of computer gaming. We now have the development of simulation of the real world, and supplementation of the real world. Mechanical simulation of the real world was developed in the Second World War, when both pilots and turret gunners were trained in simulations of aircraft environments. The use of such simulation environments was extended by the use of new ICTs to develop flight simulators, which combine computer-generated graphics with hydraulically generated orientation adjustments. Virtuality means the immersion of the human subject in a visual and, if required, also an aural environment of computer-generated stimuli. Virtuality is not currently the optimum method of learning flying, which requires the interaction of the whole body with the cabin environment as a means of controlling the movement of the aeroplane within the outer environment. To mediate this through virtuality would require mapping the subject's body movements at a level not yet attained.

The next most important use of virtuality in the short term is medical training. Polanyi took as one of his prime examples of the tacit integration of data which cannot be communicated explicitly the three-dimensional interconnection of the tissues of the human body, with medical intervention in mind. This has now been seen as one of the most important uses of virtuality in medical training. There have been three-dimensional models of the human body, once carved in wood, latterly moulded in plastic, which can be disassembled to show the interconnection of the tissues. It has been possible for some years to 'walk through' the tissues in animated films in which the tissues are shown transparently to provide depth of vision, but there are obvious limitations to this medium. Screen-based simulations can already walk through the interconnected human body with a reasonable communication of the 'three-dimensional' feel through the perspectival effect. Virtual reality will enable the full 'surround' effect to communicate the three-dimensionality more completely. A virtual tour of the body will still be a teaching aid, which does not or should not replace the learner's active integration of their actual experience. However, virtual experience of actually being 'inside' will become more important as keyhole and other forms of camera-mediated surgery develop. Whereas open surgery uses the active integration of the surgeon's knowledge of the interconnection of the tissues but at the same time to some extent makes it redundant, a virtual walk-through can be more usefully mapped onto the reality of surgery using keyhole techniques. To run ahead into the topic of the next section, it is possible that the data of whole-body scans will be amenable to conversion into input for a walk-through program. This would no longer be a teaching device but a patient-specific diagnostic aid and an intervention planning aid.

On the basis of this rapid sketch, we can return to the question of the mutual relevance of the ideas of Polanyi and McLuhan: namely, what is the implication of being able to have the feeling of 'really being there' for the development of heuristics and indwelling? We have shown that for Helmholtz, and we believe equally for Polanyi, our inner experiences *become* knowledge about the external world precisely because we rely on them as guides to action. There is a continuity between our direct senses, our use of probes and our heuristics because the process of *relying* on our inner experience as being *about* the outside world is the same in each case. For thousands of years we have used mirrors to adjust our appearance, and for a hundred years most people have easily taken to using mirrors while driving. It seems that neurologically normal humans have no resistance to feeling that the objects in the mirror are 'really there'. There is a greater degree of resistance to the feeling that a telephone conversation partner is 'really there', which perhaps reflects a variation in reliance on visual and aural experience. As our ability to perceive at a distance increases, will we come to rely on the experience to the extent of really 'being there' wherever we have extensions which provide us with possibilities of intervention and feedback on success or failure?

Probes and heuristics in the use of scanning and imaging

Scanning and imaging are areas where we 'create' what we see. Through processes of discovery and trial and error, we work out methods which allow us to create images of what we are seeking, adapted to the parameters of our perception. If the resultant images prove to be effective in our interventions in the world, we begin to rely on their 'reality' as completely as on the direct evidence of our senses. This has been described in the case of the simplest possible image, a curve:

> Take, for example, an NMR [nuclear magnetic resonance] spectrometer. A chemist can insert a substance and get an NMR spectrogram, which is in the shape of a curve (a continuous function in 2-dimensional space). The shape of this curve is taken by chemists to be a *property* of the substance – as much a property as its crystal configuration and an even more fundamental and revealing property than its color. The NMR spectrometer is thus taken as providing a basic-level understanding of some aspect of electrochemical structure. It does this *very* indirectly, in a way that is dependent on theoretical considerations of many sorts: the theory of nuclear magnetic resonance, Fourier analysis, methods for computing Fourier transforms, methods for displaying Fourier transforms, etc. The result of all this is a *curve* that makes sense in terms of basic-level perception. Because the *curve* is comprehensible, it can be used to understand something about substances.
>
> (Lakoff 1987, p. 298)

Polanyi took the process of learning to read X-rays as a basic example of the development of tacit knowing, in which the ability to discern gestalts in a confusing mass of detail and to see them as symptoms of a real condition went hand in hand with the acquisition of an appropriate vocabulary. X-rays themselves, like ordinary photographs, are not simple artefacts, but depend on the choice of exposure times to emphasise different aspects of the underlying structures. This is less obvious when fractures are being investigated: Polanyi (1958, p. 101) took his example from pulmonary X-rays, in which the phenomena of primary interest at that time, inflammation and scarring from tuberculosis, appear to the uninitiated as spiders' webs and shadows. Polanyi also worked on interpreting anomalous diffraction phenomena which arose when X-rays were used to produce images of crystals (Polanyi 1969, pp. 97–104; and see Scott and Moleski 2005, pp. 68–77). New forms of scanning and imaging rely on more complex forms of selection and manipulation of data, as Lakoff indicates. Quite apart from the manipulation and mathematical processing of the readings to produce any image at all, electroencephalography (EEG) and magnetoencephalography (MEG) require the comparison of output from hundreds of successive images to separate out the normal, underlying activity in order to produce the relevant profile of specific brain activities (event-related fields, ERF). In positron emission tomography (PET) the target activity image is paired with a control image not associated with any special activity, but actually both are normally constructed from averages of larger numbers. Functional magnetic resonance imaging (fMRI) has two levels of resolution: one weaker, which can detect the additional take-up of oxygen by activated brain cells directly; and one stronger, which measures the increased flow of blood to cells which have been activated.[4] The relatively self-explanatory final image is the result of these manipulations and also of an arbitrary choice of final coloration – arbitrary from the point of view of its being unrelated to the visual nature of the underlying phenomena, but not from the point of view of its effect on the viewer, since scales from light to dark and the normally experienced levels of warmth of the spectral colours are used to communicate the structure of the data.

As was reported earlier, drawing on the work of Patel and Groen (1991), in Polanyi's terms, experts come to see pathological states not as anomalous, but as physiologies of well-known states in which it is no longer the features that distinguish the pathology from normality which are outstanding, but any particular anomalies that might make this particular pathological state different from others of its class. In our previous discussion we were taking 'seeing' in the wider metaphorical sense, but it can also be applied to visual seeing, and not only to the direct observation of the person or object in question, but to artefactual scans and images, when these reveal 'at a glance' that some anomalous element is present. The repertoire of new scanning and imaging techniques adds to the phenomena which can in this sense be experienced as 'anomalies', instantly alerting the specialist to the presence or absence of some indicator in a way which alters their judgement of the diagnosis or prognosis required.

8 Conclusion

The interface of innovation

We have identified four ways in which the new interpretation of Michael Polanyi's concept of the tacit component of skills and knowledge in use is relevant to Schumpeterian ideas of entrepreneurial innovation and to contemporary Schumpeterian-inspired ideas of competitive advantage and innovative collaboration:

1   We have suggested that the improvement of the tacit component of skills is part of the input into maintaining competitive advantage through continuous incremental improvement of products and processes. The analysis and marginal variation of the elements of the tacit component can itself be part of the process of continuous development of new improvements. There can also be value in developing the tacit component of the processes of routinised innovation and of routinised development of new work routines and new work teams itself. All of these factors can also play a role in the relationship of partners within the supply and value chain, within joint development projects and within major construction or exploitation projects. That is to say, a large part of the communication problems within partnerships and between stages on the supply chain arise from unanalysed differences in the profile and treatment of the tacit component.

2   In some markets it will be necessary to map and analyse the tacit component of using or servicing the goods produced in order to improve the chances of take-up and acceptance in the target market, leading to improved market share and possibly also to the acquisition of the position as standard-setter for the industry with consequential gains in ease of developing new variants on the standard. This is particularly relevant to the producers of equipment and materials within industrial sectors, but has an equivalent relevance to the producers of domestic equipment and materials and to sectors whose products are used in both economic and private life, in the first place computers and vehicles.

3   The tacit component of entrepreneurial skills and knowledge needs to be mapped and analysed. This is especially true for 'routinised' innovation processes, since rapid change in markets and technologies can require

updating skills, a process which is always incomplete if only the explicit elements of skills are addressed. It is also necessary to consider whether the situation on markets means that entrepreneurial tacit knowledge is being more rapidly eroded than expected and, if so, whether this is simply due to more rapid market change or to a failure of the known channels of information to reflect new kinds of information.

4   This leads into the more general problem of whether the tacit component of the skills of the wider workforce, or of consumers, is affected by switches in dominance between different media and whether the 'same' data presented through different media have the 'same' effect on users. The effect of safety information, product descriptions and price comparisons could all be altered by the nature of the media or by being presented in different 'bundlings' which alter the receptivity of the user.

We have suggested that all of these factors lead to increasing pressure on producers to move into client-facing market positions in order to benefit from the maximum feedback from lead clients and the leading sectors of mass markets, and to alter the dynamics of their business in order to absorb the information from the most dynamic sectors of their markets. The dynamic generally recognised within innovation literature – that producer and client innovation feed on and provide feedback for each other – has even more relevance for us when we take into consideration the tacit component and its role in enabling further stages of incremental improvement. The interfaces of the organisation with its most innovative clients and partners will in turn be the areas in which new tacit skills and knowledge can be generated and from which they can be diffused within and, as required, beyond the organisation.

Cutting across this, we have also identified the transaction cost revolution brought about by new payment and accounting media as potentially creating many new markets for goods and services previously produced in-house, within which there will arise the potential for new cycles of innovation. Although different sectors will react in different ways, since internal administration costs are also falling, and although there are innovation winners and losers when goods and services are split apart, overall the mapping of the tacit component of many service occupations will be part of the process of developing innovation systems in the sectors opened up to entrepreneurial action by these changes.

The processes for mapping the tacit component, as we have suggested, are in their infancy. We have suggested that existing national systems of competency mapping such as those of the US, Australia and South Africa, which have based their systems of occupational classification on a detailed mapping of competencies, are the natural framework for the more detailed mapping of the tacit component within each of these competencies. This does not preclude that firms or sectors which find that their competency profile is itself in constant development will not push ahead on their own. The most fruitful area for the approach will be those interfaces where it is necessary to align the tacit component of skill and knowledge between organisations or between producers and users of new technologies. The diffusion of medical technologies and safety technologies, and the sharing of techniques within joint research and development projects, may be the most pressing cases of relevance. The approach will also be of interest to those firms which are actively using the approach of migrating their skills towards meeting the needs of their most innovative clients.

In *The Handbook of Industrial Innovation* (Dodgson and Rothwell 1994) there are no entries in the index for 'Polanyi', 'skill' or 'competency'. In the *Oxford Handbook of Innovation* (Fagerberg *et al.* 2005) there are two references to Polanyi, one to *Personal Knowledge* and one to *The Tacit Dimension*, which are mentioned by different authors in two chapters, the first by Powell and Grodal in their section 'Knowledge Transfer' within the chapter 'Networks of Innovators', and the second by Lam in her section 'Organization, Cognition, Learning and Innovation' within the chapter 'Organizational Innovation'. Both references can be situated within the discourse initiated by Nonaka and Takeuchi (1995), the first being concerned with inter-firm knowledge transfer (pp. 74–7), the second with tacit knowledge in processes of organisational change (p. 125). The index contains three references to 'skill', none relating to skill diffusion, and two references to 'competency building', which does not relate to the competencies of individuals, teams or firms, but to national systems of education and training. This seems to show that there is now no greater interest than ten years ago in the role that tacit knowledge may play in the processes of innovation, incremental improvement, and diffusion of new skills. We hope that this will be different ten years from now.

Notes

1 Introduction

1   See Polanyi 1951, 1958, 1959, 1964a, 1966, 1969, and Polanyi and Prosch 1975. The most useful book-length technical discussions of Polanyi's philosophy are Grene 1966, Prosch 1986 and Sanders 1988. Short introductions are Allen 1990 and Scott 1995. A broader picture is given by the biography Scott and Moleski 2005, which also contains the most up-to-date bibliography of Polanyi's writings. The reception of Polanyi's ideas can be followed by referring to the collective volumes *The Logic of Personal Knowledge* (1961), *Intellect and Hope* (1968), *Interpretations of Life and Mind* (1971) and *Belief in Science and in Christian Life* (1980), and the special issues of the *Journal of the British Society for Phenomenology*, vol. 8, no. 4 and vol. 9, no. 1, 1977–8. The journals *Tradition and Discovery* and *Polanyiana* are dedicated to the exploration and development of Polanyi's philosophy.
2   For the topics discussed here the important texts are Schumpeter 1939, 1961 (a translation from the German text of 1934) and 1976, together with the papers and essays collected in Schumpeter 1989 and 1991.
3   The consequences of the most recent development of Schumpeterian theory in the highly technical work of Aghion and Howitt 1998 are most easily accessed through Baumol 2002.

2   The shaping of Michael Polanyi's philosophy

1   See Mays 1978 (Piaget), Újlaki 1993 (Husserl), Gill 2000, pp. 45–50 (Merleau-Ponty) and pp. 118–19 (Wittgenstein), Gourlay 2004 (Dewey and Bentley) and Mullins 2002 (Peirce).
2   English sources on the gestalt school are Köhler 1929, Koffka 1935, Ellis 1938, Petermann 1932 and Wertheimer 1961. Our understanding of the impact of the gestalt school has been deepened by the discussion of it by Gibson 1979, on whose reports we draw without following him into the details of his own further development of the theory.
3   Polanyi's analysis of nihilism and Marxism as continuations of the dynamic of positivism has great power, and can be supported from the similar and more deeply researched writings of Tomas Masaryk (see Masaryk 1972). Polanyi's failure to situate the outbreak and outcomes of the German and Russian revolutions against the background of the psychic crisis caused by the Great War is typical of his generation, and may be ascribed to a general psychosis rather than to his personal liberal beliefs.

4 Reprinted in Polanyi 1969, pp. 3–23, the topic is developed in 'History and Hope: An Analysis of Our Age' (1962) and 'Why Did We Destroy Europe?' (1970), reprinted in Polanyi 1997, pp. 79–93 and 107–15.
5 This information has been widely available in a number of sources for many years but is now most easily accessible in Scott and Moleski 2005, chs 5–7.

3 Michael Polanyi's theory of personal knowledge

1 This should not be confused with multi-tasking, which women may find easier than men, but in which the structure of each parallel focus would still have the same structure, and in any case multi-tasking may use surplus capacity which is not available during the most demanding tasks.
2 Polanyi does not use the summary of the work of Ashby, McCulloch, Pitts and Wiener given by Hayek in his 1952 book *The Sensory Order*, presumably because he disagreed with Hayek's acceptance of what he might have thought a 'mechanistic' interpretation, despite the large degree of convergence which can be found in the structure of the underlying mechanisms posited (Hayek 1952, p. 95 sections 4.53–4.55).
3 See Scott and Moleski 2005, pp. 178–9.
4 Piaget 1928 (Polanyi refers to pp. 92, 93, 213, 215) and Lave 1988.
5 Nonaka and Takeuchi 1995; von Krogh, Ichijo and Nonaka 2000; Nonaka and Nishiguchi 2001; critical responses to this trend were Gourlay 2000 and Tsoukas 2003. Our paper 'Mapping the Tacit Component: Getting away from Knowledge Conversion', forthcoming, develops our own response, which will not be repeated here.
6 See Scott 1977.
7 See Scott 1971.
8 R.R. Lazarus and R.A. McCleary (1949) *Journal of Personality*, vol. 18, p. 191, and (1951) *Psychological Review* 58, p. 113; and C.W. Eriksen and J.L. Kuethe (1956) *Journal of Abnormal and Social Psychology* 53, p. 203. See Polanyi 1966, pp. 95–6 for more details and references. Lazarus and McCleary were not cited in *Personal Knowledge*.
9 Polanyi 1969, pp. 198–9, using G.M. Stratton (1897) 'Vision without Inversion of the Retinal Image', *Psychological Review* 4, pp. 341–60 and 463–81; F.W. Snyder and N.H. Pronko (1952) *Vision without Spatial Inversion*, Wichita, KS: University of Wichita Press; and H. Kottenhoff (1961) 'Was ist richtiges Sehen mit Umkehrbrillen und in welchem Sinne steht sich das Sehen um?', *Psychologia Universalis* 5, pp. 64–80.
10 Polanyi and Prosch 1975, pp. 41–2 and Prosch 1986, pp. 56–62 (pp. 57–9 on Ames). R.L. Gregory, the British investigator of visual perception, pointed out that Helmholtz had himself intuited the principle of the Ames room: 'Looking at the [normal] room with one eye shut, we think we see it just as distinctly and definitely as with both eyes. And yet we should get exactly the same view in case every point in the room were shifted arbitrarily to a different distance from the eye, provided they all remained on the same lines of sight' (Helmholtz cited in Gregory 1970, p. 27).
11 Ryle 1949, pp. 26–60, based on Ryle 1945. Polanyi (1966, p. 7) considered that Ryle had overworked this dichotomy, saying that 'These two aspects of knowing have a similar structure and neither is ever present without the other. This is particularly clear in the art of diagnosis, which intimately combines skilful testing with expert observation.'

12 For example Reber and Reber 2001, various entries under 'gestalt'.
13 On this see Gibson 1979.
14 Piaget 1971 and 1973, see index entries for 'gestalt'.
15 Polanyi's friend and political collaborator Friedrich von Hayek proposed a theory of knowledge that was also based on trying to achieve by other means what the gestaltists had set out to do. Hayek states:

> It might at first seem as if this empiricist character of our theory would stand in an irreconcilable contrast to the strongly anti-empiricist attitude of the gestalt school with whose arguments our theory is in other respects in close agreement. I am not certain, however, that the opposition of the gestalt school to an empiricist explanation of gestalt qualities as being 'built up' by experience from sensory 'elements' need apply to a theory which, as the theory developed here, traces all sensory qualities, 'elementary' as well as gestalt qualities, to the pre-sensory formation of a network of connexions based on linkages between non-mental elements.
>
> (Hayek 1952, p. 106 section 5.16)

Polanyi several times refers to Hayek's political and economic writings but never to *The Sensory Order*, perhaps implying that he did not like the 'empiricist character' of Hayek's ideas.
16 Polanyi lists Hefferline's articles in 1966, p. 97.
17 For popular accounts of these problems, see Sachs 1984 and Ramachandran and Blakeslee 1998.
18 Very nearly half of the book *Personal Knowledge* (1958, 428 pages) is made up of the section entitled 'The Tacit Component' (pp. 69–245 out of 405 pages of text). The twenty-two references to explicit discussion of the *tacit component* listed in the index include those for the *tacit coefficient*, which is not given a separate entry in the index but referred to *component*. In the passages where Polanyi uses the term *tacit coefficient* there is no obvious distinction intended between *coefficient* and *component*. In his subsequent books Polanyi increasingly uses the terms *tacit knowing*, *tacit powers* and *tacit integration*. The book-length discussion of his thought by Prosch (1986) does not use the term *tacit component* at all but discusses only *tacit knowing*. We consider this unfortunate both because it has led to the slide from *tacit knowing* to 'tacit knowledge' and because it has caused the neglect of the aspect of variety and changeability in the mobilisation of different tacit resources. In our opinion Polanyi seems on balance to have intended the *tacit component* to be understood as made up of a wide variety of contributory inputs which would be activated in different patterns, while the *tacit coefficient* was probably intended to signify the sum total of these inputs. Since we have found that the use of the term *coefficient* either provokes simple rejection of the usage or the expectation that a simple mathematical formula is intended, we have used *tacit component* throughout, and used *tacit element* where Polanyi might have spoken of the components of the coefficient. Several of the quotations from Polanyi reproduced maintain his original usage, however. It is our intention to find ways of mapping the tacit component, while remaining clear that this will be made up of a range of incomparable elements, so that any summative score of such a mapping would have only indicative meaning.

4 Implicit, tacit and explicit components of personal knowledge

1 See the overviews Seger 1994, Stadler and French 1998, Dienes and Perner 1999, Reber, Allen and Reber in Sternberg 1999, French and Cleeremans 2002, Shanks 2005, and the application of the theory to natural language learning in Ellis 1997.

2 This also provides a possible explanation for the access which individuals can achieve to the embedded knowledge. Whereas it would be unimaginable how individuals could access a hidden algorithm which explained the entirety of the phenomena as implicitly known to them, individuals can if they wish to investigate the matter ask themselves systematically which 'pairs' are licit and illicit in particular systems, and so can build up a database of yes–no judgements from which they can consciously construct the system of rules underlying the data. It would be important to understand that the new conscious system does not replace or absorb the old unconscious system, which remains in existence and to the use of which we presumably may revert when operating under circumstances which hinder conscious thought. If the consciously constructed system is used so often as to develop 'tacit' sub-consciousness, we may have three modes of dealing with the same phenomena and three databases, or at least pathways, with different structures.

3 Reber 1993, p. 12. Other sources which Reber thinks it worthwhile to cite as influences are the decision theory tradition as collected in Kahnemann, Slovic and Tversky (1982), and Herbert A. Simon. See also Reber 1992a and 1992b.

4 Reber 1993, p. 26. Polanyi's awareness of the process which Reber calls implicit learning is shown in a passage from *Knowing and Being*: 'Psychologists have called subception a process of learning without awareness' (Polanyi 1969, p. 143, referring to C.W. Eriksen (1960) 'Discrimination and Learning without Awareness: A methodological survey and evaluation', *Psychological Review* 67, pp. 279–300). Conversely, Reber (1993, p. 64) on the parallel with 'knowing more than we can say': 'knowledge acquired from implicit learning procedures is knowledge that, in some "raw" fashion, is always ahead of the capability of its possessor to explicate it. Hence, while it is misleading to argue that implicitly acquired knowledge is completely unconscious, it is not misleading to argue that the implicitly acquired epistemic contents of mind are always richer and more sophisticated than that which can be explicated'.

5 Estes 1994, pp. 51–5 discusses the prototype theory as being strongly represented in psychological theory but as less popular than the exemplar theory in information-processing approaches.

6 We would like to acknowledge the valuable role of the literature review on tacit knowledge and motor skills by Stephen Gourlay 2005, which covers a wider field than this section.

7 For a rare attempt to conceptualise and map how the development of organisational competence in developing new technologies is manifested in the development of individual and distributed knowledge within the organisation, see Nielsen 2001.

8 See Polanyi 1969, pp. 73–86 on the tacit element in scientific consensus, and pp. 87–96 on the initial rejection and then gradual acceptance of his own proposed theory of gas adsorption. Polanyi 1969, pp. 74–8 and Polanyi and Prosch 1975, pp. 134–5 discuss the 'Velikovsky Affair' and defend the rejection of Velikovsky's claims by the scientific community, while suggesting that there can never be a final set of explicit rules for judging a new theory implausible.

9 Polanyi 1958, p. 52 and Collins 2001, discussed by Gourlay 2002.

10 In the articles and working papers Busch and Richards 2000, 2001, 2004, Busch, Richards and Dampney 2001a, 2001b and 2003, and Busch and Richards n.d.a–d.

11 See, for instance, Johannessen, Olaisen and Olsen 2001, Mascitelli 2000, and Lu, Leung and Koch 2006.

5 The real and false relevance of economic innovation

1 Schumpeter 1961, pp. 132–6. This list is not always reproduced exactly in other formulations by Schumpeter. On p. 66 of the same work he lists only five: new goods, new methods, new markets, new supply sources and new forms of organisation.
2 Although in his extended treatment of this topic he vigorously rebutted this view (1976, pp. 117–18).
3 Schumpeter's three most important works on entrepreneurship are Schumpeter 1939, 1961 and 1976, but our understanding of his thought has been greatly influenced by the articles and speeches on related topics in Schumpeter 1989 and 1991.
4 See Laufer and Glick 1996 for a description of the induction of salesmen into the operations of such a market, that for industrial supply of nuts, bolts and screws, which involves selling, sourcing, buying and pricing.
5 Hayek 1978, p. 179 n. 2 and Kirzner 1973, pp. 84–7.
6 Schumpeter cannot see the distinction between usurious and non-usurious interest in the same light as any other economists, because of his fundamental assertion that the processes which channel savings into innovative entrepreneurial activity are unique to modern capitalism.
7 See Boisot 1998, pp. 234–40 on the difficulty of retrieving tacit knowledge from failed projects, using an example from Courtaulds' fibre development.
8 Based on the US editions (1962 and 1967, respectively) of Polanyi 1958 and 1966.
9 'Skillful acts of selection from the available options are constituents of the main skill itself: they are "choices" embedded in a capability. Deliberate choice plays a narrowly circumscribed role, limited under normal circumstances to the selection of the large-scale behavior sequence to be initiated' (Nelson and Winter 1982, pp. 84–5).
10 See the distinction between aggressive and defensive innovation strategies developed by Freeman and Soete 1997, pp. 268–85.
11 They introduce the concept on pp. 35–6, saying that they 'accept and absorb into our analysis many of the ideas of the behavioral theorists', citing Simon, Cyert and March. The passage discussed here is one of the instances of the use of this approach.
12

> These two kinds of awareness – the subsidiary and the focal – are fundamental to the tacit apprehension of coherence. Gestalt psychology has demonstrated that when we recognise a whole, we see its parts differently from the way we see them in isolation. It has shown that within a whole its parts have a functional appearance which they lack in isolation and that we can cause the merging of the parts in the whole by shifting our attention from the parts to the whole.
> (Polanyi 1969, p. 140)

13 Especially North (1990), Williamson and Winter (1991), Langlois and Robertson (1995), Williamson (1996), Whitley and Kristensen (1997), Dosi, Teece and Chytry (1998), Lane and Bachmann (1998), and Swann, Prevezer and Stout (1998).

14

> This social function [that of the entrepreneur] is already losing importance and is bound to lose it at an accelerating rate in the future even if the economic process itself of which entrepreneurship was the prime mover went on unabated. For, on the one hand, it is much easier now than it has been in the past to do things that lie outside familiar routine – innovation itself is being reduced to routine. Technological progress is increasingly becoming the business of teams of trained specialists who turn out what is required and make it work in predictable ways. The romance of earlier commercial adventure is rapidly wearing away, because so many more things can be strictly calculated that had of old to be visualised in a flash of genius.
>
> (Schumpeter 1976, p. 132)

15 It is arguable that it is only during the last fifty years that private automobile ownership has become a global phenomenon, and is only now reaching some parts of the world, which opens the question of the 'staggering' of waves, regarded in their purely technological sense, across the different geopolitical blocs.
16 This could be a result of the dominance of military concerns in 'big' science and technology research, which in turn greatly helps to explain the 'success' of Japan in consumer-oriented innovation (see Kleinknecht 1987, p. 211).
17

> In particular within the ordinary routine there is no need for leadership . . . This is so because all knowledge and habit once acquired becomes as firmly rooted in ourselves as a railway embankment in the earth. It does not require to be continually renewed and consciously reproduced, but sinks into the strata of subconsciousness. It is normally transmitted almost without friction by inheritance, teaching, upbringing, pressure of environment. Everything we think, feel, or do often enough becomes automatic and our conscious life is unburdened of it. The enormous economy of force, in the race and the individual, here involved is not great enough, however, to make daily life a light burden and to prevent its demands from exhausting the average energy all the same. But it is great enough to make it possible to meet the ordinary claims. This holds good likewise for economic daily life. And from this it follows also for economic life that every step outside the boundaries of routine has difficulties and involves a new element. It is this element that constitutes the phenomenon of leadership.
>
> (Schumpeter, 1961, p. 86)

> We have seen that the function of the entrepreneurs is to reform or revolutionize the pattern of production by exploiting an invention or, more generally, an untried technological possibility for producing a new commodity or producing an old one in a new way, by opening up a new source of supply of materials or a new outlet for products, by reorganizing an industry and so on . . . To undertake such new things is difficult and constitutes a distinct economic function, first, because they lie outside of the routine tasks which everybody understands and secondly, because the environment resists in many ways that vary, according to social conditions, from simple refusal either to finance or to buy a new thing, to physical attack on the man who tries to produce it. To act with confidence beyond the range of physical beacons and to overcome that resistance requires aptitudes that are present in only a small fraction of the population and that define the entrepreneurial type as well as the entrepreneurial

function. This function does not essentially consist in either inventing anything or otherwise creating the conditions which the enterprise exploits. It consists in getting things done.

(Schumpeter 1976, p. 132)

18 '[B]eing an entrepreneur is not a profession and as a rule not a lasting condition' (Schumpeter 1961, p. 78).
19

The second reason explains why a new boom does not simply follow on: because the action of the group of entrepreneurs has in the meanwhile altered the data of the system, upset its equilibrium, and thus started an apparently irregular movement in the economic system, which we conceive as a struggle towards a new equilibrium position. This makes accurate calculation impossible in general, but especially for the planning of new enterprises.

(Schumpeter 1961, pp. 235–6)

20 Kleinknecht 1987 is a defence of the existence of Kondratieff long waves and of the viability of some aspects of Schumpeter's model as a possible explanation of them.
21 See the section 'A Final Note on Skill' in Bravermann 1974, pp. 424–47, especially pp. 427–32, where Bravermann demonstrates that much of the apparent rise in skills in the US workforce in the first half of the twentieth century was an artefact of the retrospective reclassification as 'unskilled' of the mass of workers who had no specialised trade but who generally would have had the whole range of skills necessary in rural life at the time. This has important implications for current policy regarding 'generic' skills, such as those of using ICTs, which may during the individual's lifespan undergo an equivalent devaluation.
22 '[The existing set of technologies] may be expected to shape the educational system and the training of engineers and other technical personnel. The inertial forces here may strengthen the commitment to an existing technology and render more difficult the exploration of new realms of human possibilities' (Rosenberg and Frischtak 1983 cited by Kleinknecht 1987, p. 201).
23 Stiglitz 2002, pp. 54–9 and 73–8 on complexity-reducing effects of government disengagement.

6 Tacit knowledge in the New Economy

1 Drucker 1993, p. 7; and see the entire section 'From Capitalism to the Knowledge Society', pp. 17–42. We do not take issue with Drucker's use of the term 'post-capitalist', although his postulate of the previous reality of a society based on factor payments would itself be challenged by Schumpeter, for whom the payments to these actors would always be an amalgam of reward for their productive activities, and the quasi-rents on historical innovations in so far as these had not yet been eroded by new entrants into their markets. This should not be confused with the differential profit rates earned from market segmentation, since, as Baumol has demonstrated, market segmentation is generally not the result of monopoly power but, on the contrary, the result of competition among producers in a context where different consumer groups have differential bargaining power (see Baumol on 'Discriminatory Pricing', 2002, pp. 167–71). The stock-market phenomena of the New Economy do suggest that we are witnessing the emergence of the underlying reality as Schumpeter sees it: namely, that firms are not owners but borrowers of

capital. For Schumpeter the constitutive aspect of capitalist society is that institutions exist that channel savings into innovative investment and away from rent-seeking.

2 It could also be argued, and has been by Baumol, Blackman and Wolff 1989, pp. 184–7, that there are also cultural barriers to the free movement of capital, explaining why high-saving countries retain their places as the highest-investment countries despite the attraction of higher interest rates elsewhere.

3 It could be argued that there is a social cost to transaction costs, in so far as firms are prepared to accept internal inefficiencies in excess of the transaction costs saved, since the firm is oriented to the survival of the particular firm, which may be threatened by lack of crucial supplies, while for the economy as a whole the additional transaction costs accepted by firms for this reason do not necessarily outweigh the costs of bankruptcies which would otherwise occur. This is relevant to the debate about the cultural divide between the US and Europe concerning acceptance of failure.

4 He draws on Chandler 1977 and Robertson and Langlois 1995, in which they report a similar argument put forward in Silver 1984.

5 As identified and discussed in Bianchi 1996 and Qvortrup and Bianchi 1996.

6 In this context the Austrian model of entrepreneurship and of the impossibility of 'equilibrium' would lead to revising the probability weightings of the development of the 'information society' towards either a decentralised market based on standardised information and cost competition or towards a clustered market based on non-standard information and knowledge competition in the latter direction, as innovation and uncertainty are seen not merely as results of technological innovation but as inherent (and positive) products of the market process itself (Bianchi 1996, derived from Cornford, Gillespie and Richardson 1996; see also Cornford, Gillespie and Richardson 2000). While many of the proposals discussed by Bianchi as likely to decentralise and thus distribute more evenly the developments of the information society may have some effect, the model is perhaps weakened by an underlying assumption of equilibrium which is merely disturbed by technological innovation.

7 Although Langlois 1999 develops an argument concerning the origin of the factory system which could obviously be extended to the cases of Fordism and the Japanese model, according to which these phenomena are not primarily the result of conflict between management and labour over either remuneration or control over the process, but of the imperatives of demand, requiring a re-engineering of the production process in order to meet new needs, quantitative in the first two cases, qualitative in the third.

8 Baumol has been active in developing such approaches.

9 Buckley and Chapman 1997 questions whether management estimations of transaction costs are ever anything other than intuited. The arguments developed here concerning the incomparability of production processes which are wrapped up within integrated firms may contribute to explaining why it is seldom worthwhile for managers to calculate potential transaction costs of alternative courses of action and why the extension of the market, which a reduction in transaction costs might initiate, would lead to a more calculating approach if it created a broader range of alternative courses of action.

10 In the chapter 'e-Business and the New Economy' (Castells 2001, pp. 64–115), drawing on the concepts developed earlier in the chapter 'The Network Enterprise' (Castells 1996, pp. 151–200). The information society and the knowledge society may be real stages in the evolution of society, just as cyberspace, embodied in the Internet, and globalisation, with its infrastructural, legal and technological aspects, may be real stages in fundamental processes of world unification. We focus on the

New Economy as the area in which new ICTs and the possibilities of global outsourcing have created new opportunities for entrepreneurial innovation by enabling the extension of the market into activities previously done within firms. Pressures are created which lead every firm to hone and if necessary redefine its core business. The activities which it sources from the market become the core business of other firms and are thus exposed to entrepreneurial innovation.

7 Tacit knowledge, cyberspace and new imaging techniques

1 McLuhan 1962, pp. 281–9, namely those of Chaytor, Dantzig, Febvre and Martin, Hadas, Innis, Kenyon, Lord and Ong. Parry 1971 contains works by the precursor of orality theory Milman Parry, who died in 1935, having published only in French.
2 Havelock 1963; Goody 1977, 1986 and 1987; Eisenstein 1979; Ong 1958, 1967, 1977 and 1982; Stock 1983; Lord 1991; Olson 1994; Saenger 1997. These works all take up the theme of orality and literacy in various ways. Further development of the orality–literacy debate is documented in the collaborative volumes Olson 1980; Olson and Torrance 1991, 1996a, 1996b and 2001; and Astington 2000.
3 Hogarth 2001, pp. 94–6 and the literature cited there. In terms of our preceding discussion of implicit learning, this would mean that the 'intuition' of experts could be reverse-engineered by investigating their patterns of exposure to data rather than by attempting to replicate their actual decision processes. Chi *et al.* 1989 describe the processes by which students who engage in more attempts at self-explanation of why and how operations they are learning work later perform better on analogous problems. Although they do not touch on the aspect of whether the later improvement was expressed tacitly or explicitly, they show that expertise consisted in building up a repertoire of constraints which limited the possible outcomes of future problems.
4 All examples from Gazzaniga, Ivry and Mangun 2002, pp. 129–43.

References

The philosophical works of Michael Polanyi

(1946). *Science, Faith and Society*. Oxford: Oxford University Press. Always cited from the repaginated Chicago 1964 edition (see below).

(1951). *The Logic of Liberty*. London: Routledge & Kegan Paul. Reprint 1998 Indianapolis: Liberty Fund.

(1958). *Personal Knowledge*. Chicago: University of Chicago Press.

(1959). *The Study of Man*. London: Routledge & Kegan Paul.

(1964a). *Science, Faith and Society*. 2nd edn, with a new introduction by the author. Chicago: University of Chicago Press. The new introduction is run in with the main text in a new pagination.

(1964b). 'Preface to the Torchbook edition', pp. ix–xi in *Personal Knowledge*. New York and Evanston 1964: Harper & Row.

(1966). *The Tacit Dimension*. London: Routledge & Kegan Paul.

(1969). *Knowing and Being*, ed. Marjorie Grene. London: Routledge & Kegan Paul.

With Harry Prosch (1975). *Meaning*. Chicago: University of Chicago Press.

(1997). *Society, Economics and Philosophy, Selected Papers*, ed. R.T. Allen. New Brunswick and London: Transaction Publishers.

There are bibliographies of the writings of Polanyi in *The Logic of Personal Knowledge*, 1961, pp. 239–47, Prosch 1986, pp. 319–46, and Scott and Moleski 2005, pp. 327–50.

General references

Aghion, Philippe, and Peter Howitt (1998). *Endogenous Growth Theory*. Cambridge, MA, and London: MIT Press.

Allen, R.T. (1990). *Polanyi*. London: Claridge Press.

Ambrosini, Véronique (2003). *Tacit and Ambiguous Sources of Competitive Advantage*. Basingstoke and New York: Palgrave Macmillan.

Ambrosini, Véronique, and Cliff Bowman (2001). Tacit Knowledge: Some Suggestions for Operationalisation. *Journal of Management Studies* 38, pp. 811–29.

Arora, Ashish, Farasat Bokhari and Benoit Morel (1996). *Returns to Specialisation, Transaction Costs, and the Dynamics of Industry Evolution*. Carnegie Mellon University Working Paper Series, No. 96-26.

Astington, Janet Wilde, ed. (2000). *Minds in the Making: Essays in Honour of David R. Olson*. Oxford: Blackwell.

Baumol, William J. (1993). *Entrepreneurship, Management, and the Structure of Payoffs*. Cambridge, MA, and London: MIT Press.

—— (2002). *The Free-Market Innovation Machine*. Princeton and Oxford: Princeton University Press.

Baumol, William J., Sue Anne Batey Blackman and Edward J. Wolff (1989). *Productivity and American Leadership*. Cambridge, MA: MIT Press.

Bhagwati, Jagdish (1988). Global Interdependence and International Migration, in J. Cassing and E. Husted, eds, *Capital, Technology, and Labor in the New Global Economy*. Washington, DC: American Enterprise Institute, pp. 149–83.

—— (1991). *Political Economy and International Economics*, ed. Douglas A. Irwin. Cambridge, MA: MIT Press.

—— (1997). *Writings on International Economics*, ed. V.N. Balasubramanyam. Oxford: Oxford University Press.

Bianchi, Annaflavia (1996). *New Information and Communication Technologies and Endogenous Firms in the European Periphery*. Presentation to UNU INTECH Conference, Maastricht, October.

Boisot, Max H. (1998). *Knowledge Assets*. Oxford: Oxford University Press.

Booth, Alison L., and Dennis J. Snower, eds (1996). *Acquiring Skills: Market Failures, Their Symptoms and Policy Responses*. Cambridge: Cambridge University Press.

Born, Max (1964). *Natural Philosophy of Cause and Chance*. Enlarged edition. New York: Dover.

Bravermann, Harry (1974). *Labor and Monopoly Capital*. New York: Monthly Review.

Buckley, Peter J., and Malcolm Chapman (1997). The Perception and Measurement of Transaction Costs. *Cambridge Journal of Economics* 21, pp. 127–45.

Burtt, F.A. (1932). *The Metaphysical Foundations of Modern Science*. 2nd edn. New York: Doubleday.

Busch, Peter, and Debbie Richards (n.d.a) *Modelling Tacit Knowledge via Questionnaire Data*. Department of Computing, Division of Information and Communications Sciences, Macquarie University, Sydney, Australia.

—— (n.d.b) *Tacit Knowledge and Culture*. Department of Computing, Division of Information and Communications Sciences, Macquarie University, Sydney, Australia.

—— (n.d.c) *Tacit Knowledge Diffusion via Technology and Human Networks*. Department of Computing, Division of Information and Communications Sciences, Macquarie University, Sydney, Australia.

—— (n.d.d) *The Implications of Tacit Knowledge Research for Organisations*. Department of Computing, Division of Information and Communications Sciences, Macquarie University, Sydney, Australia.

—— (2000). *Triangulated Measurement of Articulable Tacit Knowledge with an Emphasis on Formal Concept Analysis*. Department of Computing, Division of Information and Communications Sciences, Macquarie University, Sydney, Australia.

—— (2001). *Graphically Defining Articulable Tacit Knowledge*. Paper from Visualisation, Pan-Sydney Workshop on Visual Information Processing, December 2000, *Conferences in Research and Practice in Information Technology*, Vol. 2, ed. P. Eades and J. Jin, pp. 51–60.

—— (2004). *Acquisition of Articulable Tacit Knowledge*. Department of Computing, Division of Information and Communications Sciences, Macquarie University, Sydney, Australia.

Busch, Peter, Debbie Richards and C.N.G. 'Kit' Dampney (2001a). *Mapping Tacit Knowledge Flows within Organisation X*. Department of Computing, Division of Information and Communications Sciences, Macquarie University, Sydney, Australia.

—— (2001b). *Visual Mapping of Articulable Tacit Knowledge*. Department of Computing, Division of Information and Communications Sciences, Macquarie University, Sydney, Australia.

—— (2003). *The Graphical Interpretation of Plausible Tacit Knowledge Flows*. Department of Computing, Division of Information and Communications Sciences, Macquarie University, Sydney, Australia.

Castells, Manuel (1996–8). *The Information Age: Economy, Society and Culture*. 3 volumes. Oxford: Blackwell.

—— (2001). *The Internet Galaxy: Reflections on the Internet, Business, and Society*. Oxford: Oxford University Press.

Chandler, A.D., Jr. (1977). *The Visible Hand*. Cambridge, MA: Harvard University Press.

Chi, Michelene T.H., Miriam Bassok, Matthew W. Lewis, Peter Reimann and Robert Glaser (1989). Self-Explanations: How Students Study and Use Examples in Learning to Solve Problems. *Cognitive Science* 13, pp. 145–82.

Coase, R.H. (1988). *The Firm, the Market and the Law*. Chicago: University of Chicago Press.

Cohen, Robert S. (1971). Tacit, Social and Hopeful, in Marjorie Grene, ed., *Interpretations of Life and Mind: Essays around the Problem of Reduction*. London: Routledge & Kegan Paul, pp. 137–48.

Collins, H.M. (2001). Tacit Knowledge, Trust, and the Q of Sapphire. *Social Studies of Science* 31, pp. 71–85.

Converse, Patrick D., Frederick L. Oswald, Kevin A. Field and Elizabeth B. izot (2004). Matching Individuals to Occupations Using Abilities and the O*NET: Issues and an Application in Career Guidance. *Personnel Psychology* 57, pp. 451–87.

Cornford, J., A. Gillespie and R. Richardson (1996). *Regional Development in the Information Society: A Review and Analysis*. Report to the European Commission's High Level Expert Group on the Social and Societal Implications of the Information Society, CURDS, Newcastle University, Newcastle.

—— (2000). Regional Development in the Information Society, in K. Ducatel, J. Webster and W. Herrmann, eds, *The Information Society in Europe: Work and Life in an Age of Globalization*. Lanham, MD: Rowan & Littlefield, pp. 21–44.

Cullen, Joseph, Barbara Jones and Bob Miller (2001) European Movement towards a Competency-Based Skills Taxonomy and a Personal Skills Profile, in Tarek M. Khalil, Louis A. Lefebvre and Robert M. Mason, eds, *Management of Technology: The Key to Prosperity in the Third Millennium*. Oxford: Elsevier, pp. 363–72.

Dienes, Zoltán, and Josef Perner (1999). A Theory of Implicit and Explicit Knowledge. *Behavioral and Brain Sciences* 22, pp. 735–808.

Dodgson, Mark and Roy Rothwell, eds (1994). *The Handbook of Industrial Innovation*. Cheltenham: Edward Elgar.

Dosi, Giovanni, David J. Teece and Josef Chytry, eds (1998). *Technology, Organization, and Competitiveness*. Oxford: Oxford University Press.

Drucker, Peter F. (1993). *Post-Capitalist Society*. Oxford: Butterworth-Heinemann.

Eisenstein, Elizabeth L. (1979). *The Printing Press as an Agent of Change*. Cambridge: Cambridge University Press.

Ellis, N.C., ed. (1997). *Implicit and Explicit Learning of Languages*. London and San Diego: Academic Press.

Ellis, Willis D. (1938). *A Source Book of Gestalt Psychology*. London: Routledge & Kegan Paul.

Elsner, Monika, Thomas Müller and Peter M. Spangenberg (1994). The Early History of German Television: The Slow Development of a Fast Medium, in Hans Ulrich Gumbrecht and K. Ludwig Pfeiffer, eds, *Materialities of Communication*. Stanford: Stanford University Press, pp. 107–43.

Estes, W.K. (1994). *Classification and Cognition*. Oxford: Oxford University Press.

Fagerberg, Jan, David C. Mowey and Richard R. Nelson, eds (2005). *The Oxford Handbook of Innovation*. Oxford: Oxford University Press.

Freeman, Chris (1994). Innovation and Growth, in Mark Dodgson and Roy Rothwell, eds, *The Handbook of Industrial Innovation*. Cheltenham: Edward Elgar, pp. 78–93.

Freeman, Chris, and Luc Soete (1997). *The Economics of Industrial Innovation*. 3rd edn. London: Pinter.

French, Robert M., and Axel Cleeremans, eds (2002). *Implicit Learning and Consciousness*. Hove: Psychology Press.

Furth, Hans G. (1969). *Piaget and Knowledge: Theoretical Perspectives*. Englewood Cliffs, NJ: Prentice-Hall.

Gazzaniga, Michael S., Richard B. Ivry and George R. Mangun (2002). *Cognitive Neuroscience*. 2nd edn. New York: W.W. Norton.

Gibson, James J. (1979). *The Ecological Approach to Visual Perception*. Boston: Houghton Mifflin.

Gill, Jerry H. (2000). *The Tacit Mode: Michael Polanyi's Postmodern Philosophy*. Albany, NY: SUNY Press.

Goody, Jack (1977). *The Domestication of the Savage Mind*. Cambridge: Cambridge University Press.

—— (1986). *The Logic of Writing and the Organization of Society*. Cambridge: Cambridge University Press.

—— (1987). *The Interface between the Written and the Oral*. Cambridge: Cambridge University Press.

Gourlay, Stephen (2000). On Some Cracks in the 'Engine' of Knowledge-Creation: A Conceptual Critique of Nonaka and Takeuchi's (1995) Model. British Academy of Management Conference, 13–15 September.

—— (2002). *Tacit Knowledge, Tacit Knowing or Behaving?* Athens: OKLC.

—— (2004). Knowing as Semiosis: Steps towards a Reconceptualization of 'Tacit Knowledge', in Haridimos Tsoukas and Nikolaos Mylonopoulos, eds, *Organizations as Knowledge Systems*. London: Palgrave Macmillan, pp. 86–105.

—— (2005). Tacit Knowledge: Unpacking the Motor Skills Metaphor. Sixth European Conference on Organizational Knowledge, Learning, and Capabilities, Waltham, MA, 17–19 March.

Granovetter, Mark (1985). Economic Action and Social Structure: The Problem of

Embeddedness. *American Journal of Sociology* 91, pp. 481–501. Reprint in Mark Granovetter and Richard Swedberg, eds (1992). *The Sociology of Economic Life.* Boulder, CO: Westview Press.

Gregory, R.L. (1970). *The Intelligent Eye.* London: Weidenfeld & Nicolson.

Grene, Marjorie (1966). *The Knower and the Known.* New York: Basic Books.

——, ed., (1971). *Interpretations of Life and Mind. Essays around the Problem of Reduction.* London: Routledge & Kegan Paul.

—— (1977). Tacit Knowing: Grounds for a Revolution in Philosophy. *Journal of the British Society for Phenomenology* 8, pp. 164–200.

Havelock, Eric A. (1963). *Preface to Plato.* Cambridge, MA: Harvard University Press.

Hayek, F.A. (1948), The Meaning of Competition, in *Individualism and Economic Order.* Chicago: University of Chicago Press, pp. 92–106.

—— (1952). *The Sensory Order: An Inquiry into the Foundations of Theoretical Psychology.* London: Routledge & Kegan Paul.

—— (1962). Rules, Perception and Intelligibility. *Proceedings of the British Academy* 48, pp. 321–44.

—— (1978). Competition as a Discovery Procedure, in *New Studies in Philosophy, Politics, Economics, and the History of Ideas.* London: Routledge, pp. 179–90.

Henkel, Joachim, and Eric von Hippel (2003). *Welfare Implications of User Innovation.* CEPR Discussion Paper 4063.

Hertz, Paul, and Moritz Schlick (1977). Hermann von Helmholtz in *Epistemological Writings*, trans. Malcolm F. Lowe; ed., with an introduction and bibliography, Robert S. Cohen and Yehuda Elkana. Boston Studies in the Philosophy of Science 37. Dordrecht and Boston: D. Reidel.

Hippel, Eric von (1988). *The Sources of Innovation.* New York and Oxford: Oxford University Press.

Hodges, H.A. (1944). *Wilhelm Dilthey, an introduction.* London: Kegan Paul, Trench, Trübner & Co.

Hogarth, Robin M. (2001). *Educating Intuition.* Chicago: University of Chicago Press.

Huxley, Thomas Henry (1895/6) Hume, in *English Men of Letters.* London and New York: Macmillan.

Johannessen, Jon-Arild, Johan Olaisen and Bjørn Olsen (2001). Mismanagement of Tacit Knowledge: The Importance of Tacit Knowledge, the Danger of Information Technology, and What to Do about It. *International Journal of Information Management* 21, pp. 3–20.

Kahnemann, Daniel, Paul Slovic and Amos Tversky, eds (1982). *Judgement under Uncertainty: Heuristics and Biases.* Cambridge: Cambridge University Press.

Kirzner, Israel M. (1973). *Competition and Entrepreneurship.* Chicago: University of Chicago Press.

—— (1992). *The Meaning of Market Process.* London and New York: Routledge.

Kleinknecht, Alfred (1987). *Innovation Patterns in Crisis and Prosperity: Schumpeter's Long Cycle Reconsidered.* London: Macmillan.

Knowlton, Barbara J. (2005). Cognitive Neuropsychology of Learning and Memory, in Koen Lamberts and Robert L. Goldstone, eds, *Handbook of Cognition.* Thousand Oaks, CA: Sage, pp. 365–81.

Koffka, K. (1935). *Principles of Gestalt Psychology.* London: Kegan Paul, Trench, Trübner & Co.

Köhler, W. (1929). *Gestalt Psychology*. New York: H. Liveright.

Lakoff, George (1987). *Women, Fire, and Dangerous Things*. Chicago: University of Chicago Press.

Lam, Alice (2005). Organizational Innovation, in Jan Fagerberg, David C. Mowey and Richard R. Nelson, eds, *The Oxford Handbook of Innovation*. Oxford: Oxford University Press, pp. 115–47.

Lane, Christel, and Reinhard Bachmann, eds (1998). *Trust within and between Organisations*. Oxford: Oxford University Press.

Langford, Thomas A., and William H. Poteat, eds, (1968). *Intellect and Hope. Essays in the Thought of Michael Polanyi*. Durham, NC: Duke University Press.

Langlois, Richard N. (1995). Do Firms Plan? *Constitutional Political Economy* 6, pp. 247–61.

—— (1999). The Coevolution of Technology and Organization in the Transition to the Factory System, in Paul L. Robertson, ed., *Authority and Control in Modern Industry*. London: Routledge, pp. 45–72.

—— (2001). Knowledge, Consumption, and Endogenous Growth. *Journal of Evolutionary Economics* 11, pp. 77–93.

Langlois, Richard N., and Paul L. Robertson (1995). *Firms, Markets and Economic Change*. London: Routledge.

Laufer, Edith A., and Joseph Glick (1996). Expert and Novice Differences in Cognition and Activity: A Practical Work Activity, in Yrjö Engeström and David Middleton, eds, *Cognition and Communication at Work*. Cambridge: Cambridge University Press, pp. 177–98.

Lave, Jean (1988). *Cognition in Practice*. Cambridge: Cambridge University Press.

Levin, Richard C., Alvin K. Klevorick, Richard R. Nelson, Sidney G. Winter, Richard Gilbert and Zvi Griliches (1987). Appropriating the Returns from Industrial Research and Development. *Brookings Papers on Economic Activity* 3, Special Issue on Economics, pp. 783–831.

The Logic of Personal Knowledge: Essays Presented to Michael Polanyi on His Seventieth Birthday 11th March 1961 (1961). London: Routledge & Kegan Paul.

Lord, Albert Bates (1991). *Epic Singers and Oral Tradition*. Ithaca: Cornell University Press.

Lu, Lin, Kwok Leung and Pamela Tremain Koch (2006). Managerial Knowledge Sharing: The Role of Individual, Interpersonal, and Organizational Factors. *Management and Organization Review* 2, 1, pp. 15–41.

McLuhan, Marshall (1962). *The Gutenberg Galaxy*. Toronto: University of Toronto Press.

Marshall, Alfred (1920). *Principles of Economics*. 8th (variorum) edn. London: Macmillan.

Masaryk, Tomas G. (1972 [1898]). *Masaryk on Marx. An Abridged Edition of T.G. Masaryk, The Social Question: Philosophical and Sociological Foundations of Marxism*, ed. and trans. Erazim Kohák. Lewisburg: Bucknell University Press.

Mascitelli, Ronald (2000). From Experience: Harnessing Tacit Knowledge to Achieve Breakthrough Innovation. *Journal of Production Innovation Management* 17, pp. 179–93.

Mays, Wolf (1978). Michael Polanyi: Recollections and Comparisons. *Journal of the British Society for Phenomenology* 9(1), pp. 44–55.

Mises, Richard von (1968). *Positivism: A Study in Human Understanding*. Corrected edn. New York: Dover.

Mowery, David C., and Nathan Rosenberg (1998). *Paths of Innovation: Technological Change in 20th-Century America*. Cambridge: Cambridge University Press.

Mullins, Phil (2002). Peirce's Abduction and Polanyi's Tacit Knowing. *Journal of Speculative Philosophy* 16, 3, pp. 198–224.

Nelson, Richard R. (1996). *The Sources of Economic Growth*. Cambridge, MA, and London: Harvard University Press.

Nelson, Richard R., and Sidney J. Winter (1982). *An Evolutionary Theory of Economic Change*. Cambridge, MA: Harvard University Press.

Nielsen, Anders Paarup (2001). Capturing Knowledge within a Competence, in Tarek M. Khalil, Louis A. Lefebvre and Robert M. Mason, eds, *Management of Technology: The Key to Prosperity in the Third Millennium*. Oxford: Elsevier, pp. 481–9.

Nonaka, Ikujiro, and Hirotaka Takeuchi (1995). *The Knowledge-Creating Company*. New York: Oxford University Press.

Nonaka, Ikujiro, and Toshihiro Nishiguchi, eds (2001). *Knowledge Emergence*. Oxford: Oxford University Press.

Norman, Donald A., and Tim Shallice (1986). Attention to Action: Willed and Automatic Control of Behaviour, in R.J. Davidson *et al.*, eds, *Consciousness and Self-Regulation*, Volume 4. New York: Plenum. Reprint in Michael S. Gazzaniga, ed. (2000), *Cognitive Neuroscience: A Reader*. Oxford: Blackwell, pp. 376–90.

North, Douglass C. (1990). *Institutions, Institutional Change and Economic Performance*. Cambridge: Cambridge University Press.

Olson, David R. (1994). *The World on Paper*. Cambridge: Cambridge University Press.

——, ed. (1980). *The Social Foundations of Language and Thought: Essays in Honor of Jerome S. Bruner*. New York: Norton.

Olson, David R., and Nancy Torrance, eds (1991). *Literacy and Orality*. Cambridge: Cambridge University Press.

——, eds (1996a). *Modes of Thought*. Cambridge: Cambridge University Press.

——, eds (1996b). *The Handbook of Education and Human Development*. Oxford: Blackwell.

——, eds (2001). *The Making of Literate Societies*. Oxford: Blackwell.

Ong, W.J. (1958). *Ramus, Method, and the Decay of Dialogue*. Cambridge: Cambridge University Press.

—— (1967). *The Presence of the Word*. New Haven: Yale University Press.

—— (1977). *Interfaces of the Word*. Ithaca: Cornell University Press.

—— (1982). *Orality and Literacy*. London and New York: Methuen.

Parry, Milman (1971). *The Making of Homeric Verse*, ed. Adam Parry. Oxford: Oxford University Press.

Patel, Vimla L., and Guy J. Groen (1991). The General and Specific Nature of Medical Expertise, in K. Anders Ericsson and Jacqui Smith, eds, *Toward a General Theory of Expertise*. Cambridge: Cambridge University Press, pp. 93–125.

Pavitt, Keith (1994). *Key Characteristics of Large Innovating Firms*, in Mark Dodgson and Roy Rothwell, eds, *The Handbook of Industrial Innovation*. Cheltenham: Edward Elgar, pp. 357–66.

Penrose, Edith (1995 [1959]). *The Theory of the Growth of the Firm*. 3rd edn. Oxford: Oxford University Press.

Petermann, Bruno (1932). *The Gestalt Theory and the Problem of Configuration*. London: Kegan Paul, Trench, Trübner & Co.

Peterson, Norman G., Michael D. Mumford, Walter C. Borman, P. Richard Jeanneret and Edwin A. Fleishman (1995). *Development of Prototype Occupational Information Network (O*NET)*. 2 volumes. Utah Department of Employment Security.

—— eds (1999). *An Occupational System for the 21st Century: The Development of O*NET*. Washington, DC: American Psychological Association.

Peterson, Norman G. *et al.* (2001). Understanding Work Using the Occupational Information Network (O*NET): Implications for Practice and Research. *Personnel Psychology* 54, pp. 451–92.

Piaget, Jean (1928). *Judgement and Reasoning in the Child*, trans. Marjorie Warden. London: Kegan Paul, Trench, Trübner & Co.

—— (1971). *Structuralism*, trans. and ed. Chaninah Maschler. London: Routledge & Kegan Paul.

—— (1973 [1970]). *Main Trends in Psychology*. London: George Allen & Unwin.

Porter, Michael J. (1998 [1990]). *The Competitive Advantage of Nations*. 2nd edn. London: Macmillan.

Powell, Walter W., and Stine Grodal (2005). Networks of Innovators, in Jan Fagerberg, David C. Mowey and Richard R. Nelson, eds, *The Oxford Handbook of Innovation*. Oxford: Oxford University Press, pp. 56–85.

Prosch, Harry (1986). *Michael Polanyi: A Critical Exposition*. Albany, NY: SUNY Press.

Qvortrup, L., and A. Bianchi (1996). *Barriers to and Strategies for Effective Participation in the Information Society in the Cohesion Regions*. Report to the European Commission, DG XIII and DG XVI, Vol. 3 of the Final Report of the study *An Assessement of the Social and Economic Cohesion Aspects of the Development of the Information Society*.

Ramachandran, V.S., and Sandra Blakeslee (1998). *Phantoms in the Brain*. London: HarperCollins.

Reber, Arthur S. (1992a). The Cognitive Unconscious: An Evolutionary Perspective. *Consciousness and Cognition* 1, pp. 93–133.

—— (1992b). Personal Knowledge and the Cognitive Unconscious. *Polanyiana* 3, 1, pp. 97–115.

—— (1993). *Implicit Learning and Tacit Knowledge*. Oxford Psychology Series 19. Oxford: Oxford University Press.

Reber, Arthur, and Emily Reber (2001). *The Penguin Dictionary of Psychology*. 3rd edn. London: Penguin.

Robertson, Paul L., and Richard N. Langlois (1995). Innovation, Networks, and Vertical Integration. *Research Policy* 24, pp. 543–62.

Rosenberg, Nathan, and Claudio R. Frischtak (1983). Long Waves and Economic Growth: A Critical Appraisal. *American Economic Review* 73, 2, pp. 146–51.

Russell, Bertrand (1998). *The Problems of Philosophy*. 2nd edn. Oxford: Oxford University Press.

Ryle, Gilbert (1945). Knowing How and Knowing That. *Proceedings of the Aristotelian Society* N.S. 46, pp. 1–16 [proceedings for 1945–6; published 1947].

—— (1949). *The Concept of Mind*. London: Hutchinson.

Sachs, Oliver (1984). *A Leg to Stand On*. London: Duckworth.

Saenger, Paul (1997). *Space between Words: The Origins of Silent Reading*. Stanford: Stanford University Press.

Salomon, Gavriel, ed. (1993). *Distributed Cognitions: Psychological and Educational Considerations*. Cambridge: Cambridge University Press.

Sanders, Andy F. (1988). *Michael Polanyi's Post-Critical Epistemology: A Reconstruction of Some Aspects of 'Tacit Knowing'*. Amsterdam: Rodopi.

Schlick, Moritz (1977). Notes and Comments on Helmholtz, 'The Facts of Perception', in Paul Hertz and Moritz Schlick, Hermann von Helmhotz in *Epistemological Writings*, trans. Malcolm F. Lowe; ed., with an introduction and bibliography, Robert S. Cohen and Yehuda Elkana. Boston Studies in the Philosophy of Science 37. Dordrecht and Boston: D. Reidel, pp. 163–85.

Schumpeter, Joseph (1939). *Business Cycles*. 2 volumes. New York: McGraw-Hill. Abridged edition (1964) Rendig Fels, New York: McGraw-Hill. Reprint of the abridgement (1989) Philadelphia: Porcupine Press.

—— (1961 [1911]). *Theory of Economic Development*, trans. Redvers Opie from the 4th German edn. New York: Oxford University Press.

—— (1976 [1942]). *Capitalism, Socialism and Democracy*. London: George Allen & Unwin.

—— (1989 [1951]). *Essays on Entrepreneurs, Innovations, Business Cycles and the Evolution of Capitalism*, ed. Richard V. Clemence with a new introduction by Richard Swedberg. New York and Oxford: Transaction.

—— (1991). *The Economics and Sociology of Capitalism*, ed. Richard Swedberg. Princeton: Princeton University Press.

Schutz, Alfred (1966). *Collected Papers III. Studies in Phenomenological Philosophy*, ed. I. Schutz. Phenomenologica 22. The Hague: Martinus Nijhoff.

Scott, Drusilla (1995 [1985]). *Michael Polanyi*. 2nd edn. Grand Rapids, MI: Eerdmans.

Scott, William T. (1971). Tacit Knowledge and the Concept of Mind, in *Interpretations of Life and Mind: Essays around the Problem of Reduction*, ed. Marjorie Grene. London: Routledge & Kegan Paul, pp. 117–36.

—— (1977). Commitment: A Polanyian View. *Journal of the British Society for Phenomenology* 8, 3, pp. 192–206.

Scott, William Taussig, and Martin X. Moleski (2005). *Michael Polanyi, Scientist and Philosopher*. Oxford: Oxford University Press.

Seger, Carol Augert (1994). Implicit Learning. *Psychological Bulletin* 115, pp. 163–96.

Shanks, David R. (2005). Implicit Learning, in Koen Lamberts and Robert L. Goldstone, eds, *Handbook of Cognition*. Thousand Oaks, CA: Sage, pp. 202–20.

Silver, M. (1984) *Enterprise and the Scope of the Firm*. London: Martin Robertson.

Stadler, Michael A., and Peter A. French, eds (1998). *Handbook of Implicit Learning*. Thousand Oaks, CA: Sage.

Sternberg, Robert J., ed. (1999). *The Nature of Cognition*. Cambridge, MA: MIT Press.

Stevens, Margaret (1996). Transferable Training and Poaching Externalities, in Alison L. Booth and Dennis J. Snower, eds, *Acquiring Skills: Market Failures, Their Symptoms and Policy Responses*. Cambridge: Cambridge University Press, pp. 21–40.

Stiglitz, Joseph E. (2002). *Globalization and Its Discontents*. London: Allen Lane.

Stock, Brian (1983). *The Implications of Literacy*. Princeton: Princeton University Press.

Sveiby, Karl Erik (1997). *The New Organizational Wealth*. San Francisco: Berrett-Koehler.

Swann, G.M. Peter, Martha Prevezer and David Stout, eds (1998). *The Dynamics of Industrial Clustering, International Comparisons in Computing and Biotechnology*. Oxford: Oxford University Press.

Torrance, Thomas F., ed. (1980). *Belief in Science and in Christian Life: The Relevance of Michael Polanyi's Thought for Christian Life and Faith*. Edinburgh: The Handsel Press.

Tsoukas, Haridimos (2003). Do We Really Understand Tacit Knowledge?, in M. Easterby-Smith and M.A. Lyles, eds, *Handbook of Organisational Learning and Knowledge*. Oxford: Blackwell, pp. 410–27. Revised version in H. Tsoukas (2005). *Complex Knowledge: Studies in Organisational Epistemology*. Oxford: Oxford University Press, pp. 141–61.

Újlaki, Gabriella (1993). Michael Polanyi's Theory of Personal and Tacit Knowledge as a Phenomenological Theory of Cognition. *Polanyiana* 3, 3, pp. 11–128.

Ulph, David (1996). Dynamic Competition for Market Share and the Failure of the Market for Skilled Labour, in Alison L. Booth and Dennis J. Snower, eds, *Acquiring Skills: Market Failures, Their Symptoms and Policy Responses*. Cambridge: Cambridge University Press, pp. 83–107.

von Krogh, Georg, Kazuo Ichijo and Ikujiro Nonaka (2000). *Enabling Knowledge Creation*. Oxford: Oxford University Press.

Wagner, R., and Robert J. Sternberg (1991). *Tacit Knowledge Inventory for Managers*. (This testing system, consisting of questionnaires, checklists and an interpretive manual, was originally distributed by the Psychological Corporation of San Antonio; since the reorganisation of Harcourt Brace Jovanovich, it has been available from the authors.)

Warren, Richard M., and Roslyn P. Warren (1968). *Helmholtz on Perception: Its Physiology and Development*. New York: Wiley.

Wertheimer, Max (1961 [1959]). *Productive Thinking*. Enlarged edn ed. Michael Wertheimer. London: Tavistock.

Whitley, Richard, and Peer Hull Kristensen, eds (1997). *Governance at Work*. Oxford: Oxford University Press.

Wigand, Rolf T., and Robert I. Benjamin (1995). Electronic Commerce: Effects on Electronic Markets. *Journal of Computer-Mediated Communication* 3, 1 [online journal].

Williamson, Oliver E. (1996). *The Mechanisms of Governance*. Oxford: Oxford University Press.

Williamson, Oliver E., and Sidney G. Winter, eds (1991). *The Nature of the Firm*. Oxford: Oxford University Press.

Index

For Product Safety Concerns and Information please contact our EU
representative GPSR@taylorandfrancis.com
Taylor & Francis Verlag GmbH, Kaufingerstraße 24, 80331 München, Germany

www.ingramcontent.com/pod-product-compliance
Ingram Content Group UK Ltd.
Pitfield, Milton Keynes, MK11 3LW, UK
UKHW021438080625
459435UK00011B/295

* 9 7 8 0 4 1 5 4 8 8 0 7 5 *